The Arab Economy Today

Samir Amin

Introduction by Aidan Foster-Carter

Translated by Michael Pallis

Zed Press, 57 Caledonian Road, London N1 9DN

The Arab Economy Today was originally published in French by Les Editions de Minuit, 7 Rue Bernard-Palissy, 75006 Paris; and in English with an Introduction and Complete Bibliography by Zed Press Ltd., 57 Caledonian Road, London N1 9DN, in 1982.

Copyedited by Hilary Arnot
Proofread by Anna Gourlay and Jane Pascoe
Cover design by Jacque Solomons
Typeset by Margaret Cole
Printed by Redwood Burn, Trowbridge, Wiltshire

U.S. Distributor
Lawrence Hill and Co., 520 Riverside Avenue, Westport, Conn. 06880, U.S.A.

British Library Cataloguing in Publication Data Data

Amin, Samir

The Arab Economy Today.
1. Arab countries – Economic conditions
I. Title
330.917'4927 HC498

ISBN 0 86232 081 X

Contents

The Empirical Samir Amin: A Notice and Appreciation by Aidan Foster-Carter

Preface

The title of this introduction is deliberately chosen. It has two principal aims, both relatively modest. Positively, it provides a basic account of the many and varied works of Samir Amin; normatively, it hopes that this essentially descriptive account will encourage an awareness of the richness of Amin's thought, and promote in the reader a desire to study it at first hand.

A 'notice' is less ambitious than a 'review'. Its literal aim is to draw attention, rather than (or at any rate prior to) passing judgement. This implies no presumption that the name and work of Samir Amin are unknown in the English-speaking world. Although this was true a decade ago, the 1970s have seen most of his major recent books translated into English. Yet there are two reasons why a 'notice' may, in the present context, still be appropriate. First, the sheer scope of Amin's work precludes any full review of the depth which it undoubtedly deserves, in the limited space available. Second, as will be argued further below, there is a certain imbalance in the 'consumption' of Amin in Anglophone quarters, due, especially, to his earlier detailed empirical work, as well as to the breadth of some of his more recent articles being overlooked. On one level, therefore, the purpose here is simply to put the record straight and provide a more accurate and well-rounded picture.

Equally, an 'appreciation' is not a 'critique'. However, it should not be understood as opposing or pre-empting critical scrutiny of Amin's work (nor, indeed, does it refrain from engaging in this). Once again, it is a question of balance. Much of the recent criticism of Amin's work seems to me unsatisfactory in various ways. Not only (to recall the previous point) is there little apparent awareness of important aspects of Amin's writings; but there is also, in some of the criticism Amin has attracted, an 'all-or-nothing' approach often couched in a polemical tone whose total effect seems to me to generate more heat than light.[1] Hence the intention of an 'appreciation' is at least to ensure that criticism is more securely grounded in a less hasty and partial reading of Amin than hitherto.

Beyond this, I would indeed claim that, taken as a whole, the work of Samir Amin constitutes — in its volume, range and depth — a unique contribution to the elucidation of problems of development and under-development on a world scale; both in themselves, and in their implications for our understanding of the broader issues of theory and strategy which the existence of the Third World poses for Marxism. Doubtless others will continue to disagree. But perhaps, in future, they will at least have a fuller knowledge of what they are disagreeing with.

In some ways it is not surprising that a less than accurate view of Amin prevails. The circumstantial obstacles to gaining a full picture are considerable. For one thing, the sheer volume of Amin's *oeuvre* makes it difficult enough to keep up with his prodigious output. To date, Amin has written some 20 books or book-length studies; has co-authored, edited, or contributed to at least a dozen more; and is the author of articles and papers whose number must run into three figures. Even allowing for some mutual repetition and 'auto-plagiarism', the bulk is forbiddingly large. Nor is there any particular reason to suppose that the flow will subside in future.

A secondary problem is that neither Amin nor some of his various publishers have always been as helpful in providing the reader with maps and signposts as one would have hoped.[2] In some ways this is trivial, but not wholly so; and in any case it would not be honest if this appreciation were to omit an outburst of the frustration that everyone must have felt who has tried to find their way around Amin's work as a whole. The problem has several facets, most of which boil down to the fact that Amin repeats himself not a little. (Further details of the difficulties will be found in the Introduction to the Bibliography of Amin's writings included in this volume, which it is hoped will ensure that future readers no longer have to recapitulate the false trails and tailbacks which have confused earlier explorers.)

Thirdly, and most importantly, the translation of Amin's work into English has been uneven in at least one major respect. Although he is now primarily (and properly) thought of as a theorist, what actually made Amin's name in the first place was a whole series of half a dozen or more solid empirical monographs on the economic and social development of particular countries and regions in North, West and Central Africa. Written in French during the 1960s, only two of these (on the Maghreb, and West Africa as a whole) have been translated into English.[3] Among the works untranslated, the important study of capitalist 'growth without development' in the Ivory Coast is not entirely unknown.[4] But there seems little awareness of Amin's earlier critique of 'African socialism' in Ghana, Guinea, and Mali[5] (in the last of which he also worked as an economist for three years). And his book on the indigenous business community in Senegal — still, over a decade later, one of only a handful of empirical studies of a putative 'national bourgeoisie' — seems to be entirely ignored.[6]

Further description of these and other similar works by Amin will be offered below. For now, the point is not only the obvious one, that any consideration of Amin should look at all of his work; but also to stress that these specific case studies constitute in various ways the indispensable foundation of his subsequent and better known works of general theory. While the relationship between these two stages and levels of work is not wholly straightforward, it is nonetheless inadequate to judge either in isolation from the other.

Although the foregoing constitutes the major imbalance in Amin's 'consumption' in English, two other similar aspects should be briefly mentioned before proceeding to a more systematic and detailed study. First, it is unfortunate that of Amin's two volumes of collected articles, while that on general issues has been translated, the no less valuable compilation of materials on Africa which includes 'middle range' papers on general aspects of African development, and must rank among Amin's finest work, has not.[7] (Although several have been published individually in English here and there, the cumulative effect is not the same.) Second, it is remarkable how little response there has been to Amin's recent excursions into broader questions of social and political interest — socialism, technology, the environment, feminism, and 'cultural' matters generally.[8] While sometimes avowedly speculative, these articles are of considerable interest; they also illuminate aspects of Amin's economic theories.

The Writings of Samir Amin

Amin's output already spans a quarter of a century. As mentioned previously, there is a certain relation between chronological order and subject-matter, and a rough division between the 1960s (empirical) and 1970s (theoretical) suggests itself. Even prior to this, however, brief mention must be made of Amin's earliest and almost wholly unknown writings. These in turn are of two main kinds, each in a sense reflecting an aspect of the contingencies of Amin's biography: his Egyptian nationality, and his French education.

Although the present discussion is concerned with texts rather than with presenting a biography, it should be noted that Amin was born in Cairo in 1931, and underwent his university education in Paris where he took three degrees (Institute of Political Studies, 1954; Institute of Statistics, 1955; and his Ph.D. in Economics in 1957). This triptych already anticipates the three main facets of Amin's later work, even if subsequently now one and now another aspect has guided particular texts.

Amin's actual writings from this 'first period' (roughly, the late 1950s, i.e. in his mid to late 20s) are of two kinds. First, there are his two theses. The earlier of these (1956) is a statistical study of savings and their utilization in Egypt between 1938 and 1952.[9] The latter, Amin's prize-winning Ph.D. thesis in Economics, bears having its full title quoted: 'The structural effects of the international integration of pre-capitalist economies: a theoretical study of the mechanism which has engendered the so-called "under-developed" economies'.[10]

While this might not bat eyelids today, in 1957 — 25 years ago — such formulations were virtually unheard of. Evidently, and indeed by his own admission,[11] Amin, as early as this, had already formulated a critique of existing orthodoxies, and the elements of an alternative type of theory. Although the present writer unfortunately lacks first-hand acquaintance with this or indeed any other of Amin's work from this period, Amin's own account can be noted. Only more than a decade later, in *Accumulation on a World Scale*, would Amin return to this level of work. In the interim, and deliberately, he set out to pit the theory against 'a number of concrete analyses, with as much precision and data as possible'.[12] These studies are the subject of the next section, but evidently, for Amin, they confirmed rather than undermined his original formulations: for despite what he would now regard as 'theoretical mistakes and short-comings' in his thesis, 'my fundamental position remains the same'.[13] *Accumulation on a World Scale*, in fact, incorporates passages from the thesis, especially in detailed critique of conventional economic theory.[14]

Thus far we at least have Amin the economist: empirical, theoretical, and critical. But meanwhile the *political* dimension, already implicit in the thesis, was being explicitly vented in articles on various aspects of the current situation in Egypt and the Arab world. Samir Amin's very first publication of any kind is apparently an article in *Democratie Nouvelle* (1955) entitled: 'Where is Egypt going?'.[15] At the time, this was credited to one 'Said El Masry': the first of a string of aliases of variously Franco-Arab ethnicity — 'Pierre Dupont', 'Yves Durelle', 'Hassan Riad', 'Pierre Amon', 'Ahmad El Kodsy'[16] — whose intention at the time was no doubt to avoid the attentions of the Egyptian security services, and which have remained to confuse the bibliographer.

This was the first of a dozen and more articles surveying general or particular aspects of the Egyptian political economy.[17] Again, space and ignorance preclude detailed discussion. But, in the present context, Samir Amin's detailed concern with the actual and potential functioning of specific economic sectors and industries cannot be overlooked.[18] This concern, after lying dormant for a quarter of a century, has burst forth again in the renewed study of the Egyptian and other Arab economies which constitutes the present volume. In this, as in other aspects, and for all its diversity and development, there are important threads of continuity running through Amin's *oeuvre*.

But what of the political aspect? Evidently, it was a formative experience for Amin to cut his teeth on the inadequacies at many levels of what was then the model of an 'alternative', purportedly anti-imperialist and socialist, development path: Nasser's Egypt — Amin's first employment after completing his studies was as a senior economist with the Economic Development Organization in Cairo, from 1957 to 1960. Undoubtedly, this experience and that which immediately succeeded it — namely, three years as technical adviser for planning in Mali, then newly independent and the only avowedly 'Marxist' regime on the African Continent — prompted Amin to develop a critique of such 'socialisms' which was both penetrating and prescient. This, it will be recalled, was the era of Nkrumah's dictum 'Seek ye first the political kingdom' and numerous other false dawns. Not many commentators kept a cool head in this period, but Amin was one who did. The charge levelled against him by come-lately critics, of being in some unspecified sense an ideologist and apologist for 'national bourgeoisies' and 'state capitalism', is, then, all the more ludicrous.[19]

We turn now to Amin's writings of the 1960s which, in the main, are the aforementioned empirical works. Strictly, his first published book was probably a study of monetary and financial flows in Egypt in 1957, published (in Arabic) by the Arab League in Cairo in 1959.[20] In similar vein, his first full-length publication in French was on Mali's national accounts for 1959, published in 1961.[21]

After his first two posts as a government economist, Amin returned to University life in 1963, as professor of economics variously at the universities of Poitiers, Paris, and Dakar. It was during this period (1963-70) that he gradually came to the notice of a wider professional public (albeit still almost exclusively Francophone) with a series of solid case studies of particular countries and areas. To enumerate these, first of all 'Hassan Riad's' *L'Egypte nasserienne* (1964),[22] pseudonymous at the time, can now be seen as a link with both Amin's earlier and later concerns. In 1965, in his own name, came Amin's survey of 'three African development experiences: Mali, Guinea, and Ghana'.[23] These, of course, were at the time West Africa's three avowed beacons of socialism.

Another year, and another book. The most substantial of all Amin's empirical works is his 1966 2-volume study of the Maghreb economy:[24] a detailed analysis of Morocco, Algeria, and Tunisia, both in regard to their colonial past and recent decolonization (Volume 1), and their future development potential (Volume 2). An abbreviated and updated summary volume on the same area, *The Modern Maghreb*, appeared in 1970; this was Samir Amin's first book to be translated into English (as *The Maghreb in the Modern World*).[25]

In French, meanwhile, Amin continued to maintain his prodigious rate of production of a book a year on average.

1967 brought forth his classic study of the development of capitalism in the Ivory Coast[26] (which also provided the material for his final thesis *d'agregation*).[27] Interestingly, it was thus only in his fourth book that he first turned to study an instance of full-blown 'peripheral capitalism'. In 1969 came a slight variation: a book focussing not on a country but on a class (another thing critics have accused him of not doing), namely the Senegalese business community.[28]

The focus on a country returns in his next book (1970), although geographically Amin's gaze has shifted east and south to the limits of former French Africa: the countries of Equatorial Africa (Congo-Brazzaville, Chad, Central African Republic, Gabon and Cameroon).[29] Finally, and as if to summarize this phase of his research and its findings, in 1971 Amin produced a general survey of developments in 11 countries of West Africa: the nine which are Francophone, plus Ghana and the Gambia. This book did appear in English, in 1973; albeit under a title *Neo-Colonialism in West Africa* much inferior to the original French (which translates as *West Africa Blocked: the Political Economy of Colonization 1880-1970*).[30]

It is an impressive record, by any count: eight books published in as many years, studying in depth the structures of up to 20 countries. No brief account can do justice or even convey the flavour and force of this essential part of Amin's work. Nonetheless, there may be room for a few general observations as well as some specific comments.

Several things can be said about these books in general. Their coverage has already been indicated. By region, they span ex-French Africa in its totality, from Senegal to Chad and from Morocco to the Congo; plus Egypt, and two of the four Anglophone states of West Africa. By *regime*, they consider a variety of self-styled 'socialisms' as well as different modalities of colonial and post-colonial capitalism.

There are also common aspects to Amin's approach in these books. At one level, to reiterate, they are profoundly empirical. Not the least of their merits is that they are all highly informative accounts of the countries concerned. At times, in fact, the sheer volume of data, figures and detail make it hard to see the wood for the trees (at the opposite end of the spectrum from what might be called the 'stratospheric' Amin of, for example, *Class and Nation*).[31]

This dense volume of facts is mostly within an economic framework: these are primarily *economic* analyses in both their object and method, that is, Amin analyses economic trends and phenomena, using economic tools. Secondly and secondarily, adding depth to the former, *historical* analysis is more or less present in most of these works; the book on former French Equatorial Africa is subtitled as an 'economic history'.

Politics, on the other hand, is for the most part relatively underplayed in these works, again in a dual sense. The polity is not their principal object of analysis; and the analysis itself is not explicitly couched in political categories. One should stress 'relatively', here. Not only does the amount of political analysis (in either sense) vary from book to book; but one can see in all of them — more so with hindsight, perhaps — an implicit concern with, and relevance to the kinds of theoretical issues which would be overtly posed in Amin's writings of the 1970s. It might be helpful to try to tease out at least some of these themes, by moving now from general remarks to the particular concerns of the specific works.

As mentioned above, Amin's first three published books are all more or less concerned with the critique of avowed 'socialisms'. Admittedly, in these early writings the critique is muted in various ways: mostly implicit, couched in terms of economic appraisal, rarely strident. The exception on all counts is *Nasser's Egypt*, where Amin was protected by anonymity. In other ways too, this earliest of his works studied an 'untypical' case — that is, highly unlike the societies of Subsaharan West Africa which were to become Amin's major field of work. It will not be further considered here, save to note the decisive importance of this text to a full evaluation of Amin's overall political thought and its formation.

The first impression of *Three African Development Experiences* is of drowning by statistics: from pages 21 to 58, for example, there is a figure or table on every page. More than half the book is devoted to Mali, doubtless reflecting Amin's years of employment there: Guinea and Ghana receive briefer treatment. But the general picture which emerges is fairly uniform; and seeds are planted of themes that will sprout in Amin's later work. He is profoundly critical of what he does not yet, at least here, call 'petty-bourgeois socialism'. Essentially, if implicitly, the charge is of failing to break with existing economic patterns and frameworks, political rhetoric aside. Amin shows how these regimes all attempted, in the absence or inadequacy of investment revenues, to 'advance' via deficit financing. The only tangible product of this was, not socialism, but inflation. There was little else to show by way of economic growth, let alone social welfare or redistribution. Agriculture remained largely untransformed; industry (if any) was of the traditional type.

Amin can scarcely have been surprised when two out of these three regimes subsequently fell; nor does he regard their successors as much changed.[32] Speculatively, one might suggest that his critique of these 'inflationist solutions' in Africa paralleled the simultaneously emerging critique of import-substitution economic strategies in Latin America.[33] In both cases, beginning from avowed rejection of a colonially oriented past and its results, reforming governments mooted an ambitious alternative. In both cases, the 'alternative' failed: failed, above all, to transcend the limitations imposed by its context, which ultimately it had not challenged — in theory or practice — sufficiently fundamentally. The result, in both cases, was that a more radical critique emerged out of the debris: the dependency school (epitomized, but not monopolized, by Andre Gunder Frank)[34] in Latin America, and in Africa the further theoretical development of Samir Amin.

If the three West 'African development experiences'

received rather uneven treatment, this cannot be said of the North African trio studied in *The Economy of the Maghreb.* Not only is the latter a much deeper study, but also Morocco, Algeria, and Tunisia possess a profound regional unity of geographical and historical experience, quite non-comparable with the mere ties of 'orientation' that brought together Mali, Guinea and Ghana (the last-named not even being contiguous with the other two). Hence, the first of Amin's two volumes on the Maghreb is able to subsume the region as a whole in a total perspective, comprising natural resources, population, social structures, economic transformation, and political history. In fact 'unity' is the keynote of this work in several ways. Despite the avowedly different strategies followed by each regime — 'socialist' Algeria, monarchist Morocco, Tunisia somewhere in between — Amin stresses the similarities not only of pre-existing economic and social structures but also of results. Volume 2 compares development plans and potentials for each country, concluding that a much more far-reaching transformation is called for, of which a crucial aspect is the *integration* of the region as a whole. Here we have one of Amin's signal themes: hostility to colonial balkanization, and stress on the need for *'les grands espaces'* in order to overcome fragmentation and promote genuine development. (This recurring emphasis, it may be said, would appear to separate Amin from the otherwise similar perspectives of Clive Thomas;[35] the latter being an avowed proponent of the feasibility of 'socialism-even-in-one-small-Third-World-country'.)

Amin's next work, as stated above, finally confronts a model of *capitalism* in one country. With *The Development of Capitalism in the Ivory Coast*, he is dealing with one of the 'growth miracles' extolled in the West: an economy whose annual rate of growth averaged 9% and whose exports quadrupled in the period 1950-65. Amin does not deny these quantitative achievements, nor the corresponding changes in economic and social structures. It is rather the evaluation of the *direction* of development which concerns him. He points to such factors as: the continuing dominance of foreign capital, the absence of significant local savings, the regional imbalances, the paradoxical combination of high unemployment and a large influx of foreign labour, the pronounced rural stratification and the general slowing down of the economy from around 1965 onwards. And his conclusion is as follows:

> The Ivory Coast . . . provides an excellent case study of 'growth without development': that is to say, growth created and maintained from the outside, without the structures thus established permitting one to foresee any automatic evolution towards the further stage of self-centred national development, moved by its own internal dynamism.[36]

Here we see posed — perhaps for the first time, and certainly much more explicitly than heretofore — the assumption of Amin's fundamental problematic of 'autocentric' versus 'extraverted' development paths.

Amin turned his attention to former French Equatorial Africa with his *Economic History of the Congo 1880-1968* (1969). (The title is slightly misleading, since its actual scope is wider than Congo-Brazzaville alone.) After a short historical first part on the Congo written by the French historian Catherine Coquery-Vidrovich, Amin devotes five chapters to the Congo since 1960 and two chapters to the other four countries of the area (Cameroon, Gabon, Chad and the Central African Republic) during the same period. Again his method is totalizing, and the conclusions are becoming familiar in general: neither 'socialist' (Congo) nor capitalist (the other countries) *national* strategies can even begin to tackle the real problems of development, which can only be solved on at least a regional basis. The general tone of the book is more militant than hitherto, perhaps because the author was beginning to feel no longer alone (for the first time he cites the work of Gunder Frank and other kindred souls). At the same time, his criticisms of 'socialism' in the Congo are tempered by an awareness of the particularly rapacious and destructive impact of French colonialism there, which imposed a crippling inheritance from the point of view of any effort at transformation.

The 'statistical' side of Amin's work reaches its climax, and its marriage with his theoretical work (which we have yet to consider in detail) is finally if surreptiously consummated, in his book *Neo-Colonialism in West Africa.* Here we both review old acquaintances (Ghana, Guinea, Mali, Ivory Coast) some years on, and also see the analysis applied to the remainder of the West African francophone states (plus Gambia): Senegal, Mauritania, Upper Volta, Niger, Dahomey, and Togo.[37] In fact, apart from Senegal, which occupies nearly a quarter of the text, the four countries which he has studied previously receive most attention, the newcomers being generally limited to a dozen pages each.

The work is so constructed that each country is considered twice. The first part constructs a typology of the varieties of 'externally oriented economic development', while, in the second part, the countries are regrouped on the basis of their attempted policy solutions. Both typologies might cause some surprise to those who go by appearances. Part One distinguishes four varieties of external orientation. First the 'plantation economy', such as in Ghana up to 1950 and Ivory Coast since then ('the precocious miracle' and 'the contemporary miracle'). This is marked by a period of more or less rapid export-based growth, which, however, fails to debouch into 'self-centred growth' and sooner or later runs out of steam. Senegal would seem also to belong in this category, having set out along the same road much earlier (from 1830 onwards) and having, therefore, come up against its limits sooner — as now has Ghana, but not yet Ivory Coast.

Second is the 'enclave mining economy', whose prime exemplars in West Africa are Guinea and Mauritania. (These categories are not of course static in their application; thus a third country, Niger, will be moving into this group as its uranium begins to be exploited.) Here again, despite often rapid growth rates (Mauritania's has recently been as high as

13% p.a.) based on exports whose value is generally at least sufficient to avoid balance of payments problems, there is never any prospect of transition to an inward-looking form of development. On the contrary, the mining sector remains an enclave, and in extreme cases the economy is 'totally disarticulated'.

A third category consists of countries whose development was actively blocked or destroyed by colonialism. Amin's main example here is Dahomey (now Benin) which as an independent kingdom in the mid-19th Century was already exporting as many palm oil products as it would be in 1960. French colonialism destroyed the social structure and diverted the surplus from this trade to itself: the result has been economic stagnation, a permanent financial crisis, and political instability. Togo is also placed in this category; although here the 'blocked' development was itself colonial in origin, namely Germany's 'model colonization' which had already reached 1960s income level by 1914.

Lastly, in contrast to the foregoing varieties of under-development (understood as an active process of perverse transformation), there is also the exception which proves the rule: namely, countries which by and large remained unde-veloped by colonization. In West Africa these 'reservations', as Amin calls them, were mainly inland: Mauritania (before the iron and copper discoveries), Niger (similarly in transition, as we saw), Mali, and Upper Volta. Here, colonial-ism either failed or never tried to institute any form of under-development. Nonetheless, such countries have played an important role as labour reserves: Upper Volta has had nearly a million workers in the Ivory Coast, and Mali and Mauritania still send tens of thousands of workers to France itself.

In Part Two of *Neo-Colonialism in West Africa*, Amin discusses the various policy measures that have been attempted to cope with these situations. He distinguishes two modes of 'liberal' strategy ('liberal' in financial terms), although in the long run there is only one: some countries (Dahomey, Niger, Togo, Upper Volta), within the context of the present system, are permanently doomed to budgetary and balance of payments instability, while others (Ivory Coast, Mauritania) are for the time being less hard pressed on account of export revenues. But there is always the example of Senegal as a portent of what happens when the 'boom' is over.

The only attempted alternative to 'liberal' policies is, as we saw labelled by Amin, not 'socialist' but merely 'inflationist'. Here he returns to the trio of Ghana, Guinea and Mali, showing how, in the absence of substantial investment revenues, they all attempted to advance through deficit financing, with inevitable inflationary consequences but little else to show at the end.

Amin's general conclusions are the same as before, although perhaps stated more forthrightly. More basic than the variety he describes is the essential uniformity these countries exhibit — external orientation and dependence, to which there are no purely national solutions. Planned inward-looking economic development is only possible on the basis of 'large spaces' economically integrated. On that premise, but on that alone, West Africa's prospects are good: Guinea's bauxite and Mauritania's iron could form a basis for industrialization in Senegal, for instance.

There remains one further empirical book of Amin's from this period to be discussed, somewhat different in character from the others. *Senegalese Businessmen* (1969) is a socio-historical account of an entire class (and I mean 'entire', not a sample: Amin claims to have interviewed all of them!), the Senegalese commercial bourgeoisie. Fanon's withering contempt for the 'national bourgeoisie' as a whole[38] has perhaps tended to pre-empt concrete investigation of this class in different countries. Amin restores the balance, but although his tone is far from Fanonist — many of those interviewed, he says, became his friends — the results of his investigations largely provide empirical reinforcement for Fanon's *a priori* judgements. The Senegalese commercial classes have had their ups and downs, but in either case it has been as reagents rather than independent actors. In the 19th Century the French used them to penetrate inland and pave the way for formal political colonization. That same colonialism then turned on them in the 20th Century, when competition from '*petits blancs*' and Lebanese led to severely discriminatory measures against indigenous traders. Since 1958 their fortunes have revived somewhat, as foreign capital (large and small) has withdrawn from certain sectors as profitability declined. Yet they remain essentially weak: credit is still scarce, they depend on the market provided by the state, and very few have made the crucial leap from commerce to industry (except in the service sector). The conclusion is inevitable: there is no prospect of this class playing the role of a classical 'national bourgeoisie' in terms of accumulation and industrialization.

In itself, such a judgement was almost commonplace in radical circles a decade ago (although rarely grounded in such firm empirical and historical evidence).[39] Yet history moves on: some recent studies, especially of Kenya, have suggested that obituaries of the national bourgeoisie were written prematurely.[40] More generally, it has also been argued *contra* Amin, that capitalism's allegedly moribund state in the Third World was exaggerated. In some areas at least, the patient is said to be making a remarkable recovery. There are even those who claim that it was never ill in the first place.[41] These are important questions, to which we shall more aptly return when explicitly discussing Amin's theoretical problematic.

Before this, however, it should be noted that Amin's book on the Senegalese business class is not the only example of his work that focuses on specific and 'sub-national' topics and themes. We have not dealt with (and alas, have little space to elaborate on) the considerable volume and range of shorter pieces — articles, introductions, etc — which he has also produced. Still pursuing the correlation in Amin's output between chronology and changing levels of analysis or themes, we can say that many of his shorter pieces are 'intermediate' in this double sense. Amin would appear to have published no papers at all (remarkably enough for him) during the years 1964-66. Prior to that, as we saw earlier, his articles were nearly all about Egypt (with one signal exception, to which we shall return). From 1967 onwards, however, he evidently resumed writing in this form — and has not stopped since.

Our concern here, then, is with a number of his papers dating mostly from the late 1960s to the early 1970s. Nearly all are collected in a 1976 French volume entitled *Imperialism and Underdevelopment in Africa*[42]. Unfortunately, this has not been translated as such; although there are English versions of most (but not all) the key pieces, they are widely scattered and some are inaccessible. Generally, as the title of the compilation indicates, they are about Africa. Some papers explore specific themes: one of the earliest (1967), and untranslated, is a detailed empirical study of inter-African trade, including recommendations as to how it might be both augmented and structurally transformed.[43] Or again, a paper on population roundly declares that Africa is *under*-populated.[44] There is also Amin's substantial introduction to a book (edited by him) on modern migrations in West Africa,[45] a particularly effective example of the welding together of empirical data and theoretical argument. There are papers on the Green Revolution, Africa's food shortage, the franc zone, and indeed just about everything from slavery to the development of the Senegal river basin.[46]

Besides those already alluded to, four more stand out. Two general articles offer summary accounts of the development of capitalism in Africa, and of its historical and contemporary underdevelopment and dependence.[47] Much reproduced, these papers offer interesting typology and periodization, while probing what is general and what specific about Africa's experience. Both articles were later absorbed (typically, without notification) into Amin's subsequent major works of theory (*Accumulation on a World Scale* and *Unequal Development*, respectively).[48]

Two important articles remain. Amin's critique of the Pearson Report, in the light of two decades of 'development' in Africa (1950-70),[49] shows him at his most effective, marshalling data to make a cogent theoretical and political case for the practical bankruptcy of extraverted growth and the need for autocentrism. Finally (although actually earliest), there is his somewhat inaccessible but seminal paper on the class struggle in Africa.[50] This was originally published anonymously in 1963 in a short-lived French Third World-ist journal, and therefore presumably written while Amin was still working for the Malian Government. Here he develops an explicit critique of 'socialism' in Africa, and indeed the anti-colonial movement generally, as being principally guided (*faute de mieux*, in the virtual absence of a proletariat) by the petty bourgeoisie; to be precise, the new urban lower middle classes. Nor does Amin, unlike Fanon, look in this case to the rural masses for revolutionary salvation. On the contrary, he repeatedly stresses that 'nothing is further from socialism than primitive communism'; he calls for 'the reinforcement of small merchant production at the expense of collective forms', and insists on the over-riding need to 'break the family [*briser la famille*] and its traditions . . . to develop individualism, to free the individual from the chains of tradition.'[51]

Such a programme, in both tone and content, recalls the perspectives of a Warren more than Amin as he is usually known. Striking as this paper is, two major questions remain. How far can such views be reconciled with Amin's more general critique of peripheral capitalism? (This pertains also to a more general question of the overall consistency or evolution of Amin's thought: is it a seamless web, or are there explicit or implicit shifts of position?) Secondly: given this scenario of a non-existent proletariat, a backward peasantry, and a self-serving petty bourgeoisie, who then will be the *agent* of Amin's project of transformation at any level, from smashing the family to forging African unity? An almost plaintive comment in Amin's latest text[52] (in this volume) suggests that even now, almost 20 years on, this question of an agent cries out for an answer.

It is time to turn to Amin's major theoretical writings. The greater familiarity of at least the major works here, plus the palpable absurdity of attempting a 'potted' summary, perhaps make it permissible to be even more brief and allusive than hitherto.

The main points of reference are of course *Accumulation on a World Scale* and *Unequal Development.* Originally published in 1970 and 1973 respectively, each appeared in English some years later; there are at least a further half-dozen translations of both into different languages. It is at this point that Amin's international fame took off. Also, to add one more brief note of biography, it coincides with his assumption in 1970 of the post of Director of the United Nations African Institute for Economic Development and Planning (IDEP) in Dakar, Senegal (where he had previously held a university position). Those who by now were following Amin's ideas may, from this point on, have begun to receive them first in the form of an unceasing stream of roneo'd papers that poured off the IDEP duplicators; materials that would later form part of *Unequal Development*, for example, were circulating a year or two earlier in Dar es Salaam in the early 1970s.

What then can be said about Amin's two *magna opera?* One thing that has been said, by a careful and sympathetic critic, bears repeating:

> These two works cover virtually identical ground, and *Unequal Development* is perhaps better regarded as a second edition of *Accumulation on a World Scale* . . . Substantial passages are taken virtually unchanged from [the latter] and incorporated into [the former].

Which may be some relief to the reader, facing the daunting prospect of two works totalling over 1,100 pages! There are other difficulties too. Neither work is especially well structured. *Accumulation on a World Scale* apparently began life as lecture notes[54] (in addition to its partial 'pre-history', in connection with Amin's Ph.D. thesis). Subtitled 'A critique of the theory of under-development', for much of the time it is indeed an extremely detailed engagement with numerous aspects of 'bourgeois' economic theory in relation to the actualities of underdevelopment and the world system. It is hard to avoid the impression, as Amin 'worries' all this material, of someone trying to exorcise from his thinking the last vestiges of a body of thought which at one time he had learned all too well. (To take just one example, monetary mechanisms alone are the subject of a chapter of nearly 100 pages.)[55]

All in all, *Accumulation on a World Scale* was very much a book for the economist. Perhaps wishing to reach a wider social science audience and public, *Unequal Development* has relatively less economic and more 'sociological' material (although it sorely lacks an analytical contents list). Beginning with a part schematic, part historical account of pre-capitalist modes of production and social formations (also published as a separate article),[56] successive chapters revert to broadly economic accounts of central capitalism, international aspects (including unequal exchange), and the creation and growth of peripheral capitalism. The final chapter is a more sociological account of the contemporary periphery (distinguished by region), and concludes by broaching broader questions on the question of 'transition'.

Despite the problem of having no specific footnotes (it is self-styled an 'essay'), *Unequal Development* remains the most accessible account of the mature Amin's general positions. It is also, like *Accumulation on a World Scale*, avowedly a work of synthesis; in other words, at some level these books can be taken to 'represent' not only Amin but the 'rise to maturity' of an entire school, variously characterized as 'theories of underdevelopment' or 'dependency'.

Amin's fundamental theses have been brilliantly summarized — better than he does it himself, and more succinctly than one would have thought possible — by Cheng Ngai-Lung in a work which unfortunately remains unpublished.[57] (The following is a slightly formalized and paraphrased version of her account.)

1) The world capitalist system, consisting of social formations in the centre and the periphery, is integrated into

a single world system primarily through relations of exchange and unequal specialization of production;
2) There exists in this global system a hierarchial structure of modes of production/sectors, with uneven productivity and heterogeneous relations of production;
3) Modes of production/sectors of the periphery are: (a) articulated with capitalist social formations at the centre, but (b) disarticulated with respect to social formations at the periphery;
4) This structure of articulation/disarticulation is the result of the centuries-old evolution of forms of international specialization, dictated by the internal dynamics of capitalist social formations and imposed on the periphery by the centre — initially through political domination, and subsequently through the mechanism of unequal exchange;
5) Transfer of value/economic surplus takes place from peripheral capitalist to central social formations as a result of primitive accumulation. This process survives the pre-history of capitalism; its persistence to the present constitutes the essence of the problem of accumulation on a world scale.

There is little essential which this remarkable summary fails to state. Here is the insistence on the analytical primacy of the global level, in practice constituted through unequal exchange and *continuing* 'primitive' accumulation (here Amin reformulates Emmanuel's[58] concept of 'unequal exchange'). Here, too, is Amin's basic distinction between 'centre' and 'periphery', which we should elaborate at least a little. As it happens, the 'pure' model, implicitly at the heart of *Accumulation on a World Scale* and *Unequal Development* is expounded more directly than in either book in a much cited paper, 'The theoretical model of accumulation and development in the contemporary world'.[59] Structurally, the 'central' *formation* is an organic whole, dynamized by mass demand; for Amin it also tendentically corresponds to the capitalist mode of *production*. The 'extraverted' periphery lacks such an organic link, being principally fuelled by the external demand which created it as a periphery. Moreover, — or is it the same point, made a different way? — the development of the capitalist mode of production in the periphery is structurally incomplete: pre-capitalist sectors not only survive but are functional for the system. Hence, the characteristic peripheral 'distortions' as Amin calls them: incomplete proletarianization, 'marginality' of the masses, light industry only, and others.

There is much else of interest in these two works, for example, on periodization, on the detail of different peripheral experiences (by continent and region) and so on. Travesty though it is, we have 'noted' and must pass on. Amin has subsequently not only developed these themes further but expanded his range of concerns. For analytical convenience, we shall continue to distinguish his more specifically economic contributions from more recent *excursus* into political and social aspects of theory. On this basis, two further major and some minor works of principally economic focus must be mentioned.

We have already alluded to the place of 'unequal exchange' in Amin's schema. This was the topic of a short and highly formal book published in 1973, and rather immodestly titled '*End of a Debate*'.[60] (Amin does nothing to endear himself to critics by adopting, here and elsewhere,[61] the intrinsically implausible notion that *any* question of Marxism and social science should be seen as having been 'settled', whether by him or anyone else.) This was later included in Amin's general volume of papers, translated into English as *Imperialism and Unequal Development*. The latter volume also includes a number of other pieces whose focus is principally economic. Often first published as introductions to collections or prefaces to other people's monographs, these discuss *inter alia* 'project appraisal', ground rent, and (again) international trade.[62] (Amin's version of unequal exchange is well discussed by Brewer).[63]

Samir Amin's final 'economic' work to which we have to allude is his quite short book *The Law of Value and Historical Materialism* (1977, 1978).[64] Although billed as a contribution to general aspects of Marxist theory and method, much of its substance is, in fact, a strictly economic and formal account of the mechanisms involved in for example, ground rent (again), the 'transformation problem', and even 'the theory and practice of mining rent'. Around this, however, are some rather heterogeneous chapters in which Amin not only conducts an increasingly strident polemic against various 'revisionists' and critics, but also seeks to establish an 'objective' basis for such backsliding in a global analysis of economic classes founded on a strictly reaffirmed law of value. The issues this raises may more appropriately be discussed in the next section, which considers the more general contribution made by Amin to Marxism as social theory.

It is perhaps possible to trace, in Amin's developing work, a two-stage process of 'coming out'. The first, we have seen, was the crystallization of a *theory* of economic development and underdevelopment, arising out of his earlier empirical case studies of blocked development. Now, on and within the plane of theory itself, we can see how in recent years he broaches ever more explicitly broader questions of politics and indeed of method. It is not always easy to separate these.

Already in the first chapter of *Unequal Development*, for example, we find an ambitious reformulation of traditional 'stage' theories of modes of production. The major outcome is to subsume feudalism under a broader category, the 'tributary' mode of production, which also includes such variants as the notorious 'Asiatic' mode.[65] More recently, in Amin's latest (at the time of writing) major book *Class and Nation*, this has been further developed as a reconstructed stage theory, multilinear in character, whereby all societies go through one or another of three broad 'families' of modes of production — communal, tributary, and capitalist.[66]

Or again, there is Amin's challenging idea that the periphery, being structurally unable to 'catch up' with the centre, is forced to surpass it. This too, for Amin, is a general law of historical development: in its time feudalism, too, grew up on the periphery of the civilizations of classical antiquity and their successors.[67]

What is at issue in formulations of this kind? Evidently, insofar as they bear on historical interpretation they can be judged accordingly. There seems no reason to rule out *a priori* the, at least, heuristic value of such ideas; even if it is hard to envisage what would constitute their definitive 'settlement'. But more than historical understanding is at stake. As becomes clear above all in *Class and Nation*, Amin is self-consciously fighting a political battle on several fronts.

Partly, it is a battle for the 'soul' of Marxism. As such, it is often conducted in terms, and by appeal to criteria, which are remarkably orthodox, considering the innovativeness or even heterodoxy of some of Amin's substantive contributions. Thus, Amin finds it crucially important to identify himself with what he evidently conceives as the true Papal line of Marxist succession, via Lenin and Mao, giving due weight to imperialism and (hence) national liberation, as key driving forces of the anti-capitalist struggle in the conditions thrown up by the 20th Century.[68]

Equally, he deems it no less important (as mentioned above) to construct an 'objective' basis for all these trends. This entails, amongst other things, not only virtually deducing his critics' revisionism from their participation in the fruits of unequal exchange,[69] but also more generally in *Class and Nation* totting up the global battalions in what purports to be a table of 'world income distribution' on the basis of international transfers of surplus value.[70]

It may be apparent that I think Amin has gone astray here, giving a golden opportunity to the very critics whom he wishes to combat.[71] For one thing, *Class and Nation* is for the most part pitched at such a stratospheric level of generality that it is hard to see how *anything* could be 'established' on this basis. More importantly, Amin's method here seems to me to be misguided. He tries to do both too much and too little. It is neither necessary nor possible to *reduce* political-analytical disagreements so crudely to different class forces, nor these class forces themselves so mechanically to senders or receivers of alleged quantitative flows hither and thither. For all his critique of economism, Amin remains extraordinarily reductionist in his reflexes; just as, for all his analytical openness and daring[72] — entirely admirable, justifiable, and Marxist — towards new facts and trends, he remains at a deeper level excessively fideistic. A Luther in some respects, he attacks Pope and Vatican — or rather, *this* Pope, *this* Vatican. It is not, alas, that he wants these not to be; Amin wants them to be — somewhere else, someone else.

Whether or not Amin will subsequently feel moved to purge his Marxism of Vaticanist tendencies altogether remains to be seen. But it is hard not to conclude that with *Class and Nation* he has reached (or passed beyond) the outer limits of further development — at least, in this direction. What would constitute further progress? In general, a recognition that neither political processes nor class action can profitably be analysed very far in the reductionist terms here used by him.

Fortunately, there is evidence elsewhere in his work that Amin is not only aware of the need for analyses explicitly focussed on politics and class, but is himself quite capable of making a valuable contribution in this regard. The obvious reference point here is his book *The Arab Nation* (1976, 1978)[73] : a text which does not slot easily into the major categories of Amin's work, but which is important both in itself, and especially in connection with the themes of his subsequent work on the contemporary Arab economy included in the present volume. Here Amin allies historical and theoretical discussion to the recent political history of the countries of the region, which he conceives of as potentially able to move towards an 'autocentric Pan-Arab development' under working-class leadership.[74]

While work on this level is by far preferable to the difficult generalities of *Class and Nation*, I would venture the opinion that methodologically, in one particular respect, Amin still has further to go. It seems to me that the 'national question' — which, I agree with Amin, is of vital salience for Marxism — will not even be posed, let alone resolved, without a return to a very different tradition in Marxism which gives due weight (analytically and *methodologically*) to real human beings' perception of and action upon their world.[75]

Evidently, in such a view, it is the terrain on which Amin chooses to fight, rather than his particular position on it, which is itself deemed faulty. It follows that I believe many of his critics are no less at fault in contesting this terrain. But before moving on to examine some of the criticism in more detail, we should conclude our brief survey of Amin's work to date by just mentioning some of his more particular themes.

Amin as social theorist has recently meditated on a number of issues; ranging from the fairly specific (education, technology, the environment), to broader questions: 'universality and cultural spheres', 1984, socialism itself.[76] In some of these writings a rather different Samir Amin seems to emerge: profoundly anti-capitalist *per se*, socialist, humanist; a critic of the *cultural* dehumanization brought about by capitalism, even (especially) in its 'central' form. Nor can this be reduced — as critics might wish — to just another manifestation of Third World or 'Narodnik' nostalgia for rural *gemeinschaft* and the simple life. That is not Amin's tone at all. His vision of communism may well be utopian; but it is neither more nor less so than that of Marx himself.[77]

Amin and His Critics

It was to be expected that the elaboration of such an ambitious synthesis as Amin's would attract critical attention. What was perhaps less predictable was the form that this would take. With a few distinguished exceptions, most critics of Amin seem to me to have left something to be desired. Generally, they have not considered his work as a whole. Then, having seized on this or that 'error' on the basis of a restricted reading, they jump to the conclusion that the entire edifice is (or should be) destroyed. Finally, some add insult to injury by 'explaining' his errors as flowing from various deviations: ideologist of the 'national bourgeoisie', Third Worldism, and so on.

These days, Amin gives back as good as he gets, and then some.[78] The air is thick with smoke. Foolhardy, no doubt, is he who would still like to rush in, pull the adversaries apart, and maybe knock their heads together to bring them to their senses. The wrath of both parties may descend upon him; by now, it appears, they simply want to be left to get on with their war in peace. Yet it is hard to resist the conclusion that the issues are not *quite* so polarized as both Amin and his critics are now making out. Let us see if we can briefly unravel some themes.

One might say that things got off on the wrong footing, and that Amin was quite early on the victim of a largely unprovoked assault. The first substantial consideration of him launched straight in on an unpromising note. Jean-Pierre Olivier's massive two-part article was entitled 'Africa: who exploits whom? On Samir Amin and the African state bourgeoisies'.[79] Strangely insubstantial for all its bulk, Olivier's message was in essence to characterize Amin as an implicit ideologist of the aforesaid bourgeoisies. Given the facts of Amin's early formation, and the texts of his writings (not least the case studies), this has always seemed to me the most implausible of views. It is, therefore, hardly surprising (although it peeved Olivier) that Amin 'replied' in three pages to his own seventy.[80]

That set the tone for much subsequent 'debate', as witness this recent unsparing judgement:

> Why is Amin taken seriously? . . . Amin provides a pseudo-scientific justification for a political position which is nationalistic, simplistic, and economistic. . . . All ills of all Third World countries are attributable to imperialism . . . Thus he supports the crudest kind of Third Worldism .[81]

For good measure, the same author concludes by tarring Amin with Pol Pot's brush: 'The tragedy of Kampuchea is a bitter example of where this kind of reasoning might lead.'[82]

I doubt that Amin (or indeed anyone) deserves this kind of treatment. Yet there are real or apparent problems at various levels in Amin's work, which should be distinguished from the name-calling. For convenience we can divide these into 'errors' of mathematics, logic, method, theory, substance, and fact.

The first can be rapidly disposed of. Anyone working in the Marxist (or any other) economic tradition, and hence handling quantitative concepts, not only has to confront old familiar difficulties (for example, Marx's 'transformation problem') in this sphere but may also produce new ones. In this respect Brewer has identified inconsistencies in Amin's account of autocentric accumulation.[83] However, just as no one would advocate a root and branch rejection of Marx simply because not all his equations are readily soluble, so Brewer allows that 'the arguments that I criticize . . . can be removed by surgical excision without destroying the whole'.[84]

Strictly, mathematics is but a formalized branch of logic (*pace* J.S. Mill). It seems convenient, however, to distinguish it here from more general, lower-level logical problems. Looming large for some of Amin's critics is the problem of *contradiction:* not in the Marxist sense, but simple inconsistency. Thus Bernstein, in the course of a major assault on 'radical underdevelopment theory' and all its works, picks out apparently contradicting conceptualizations in different passages of *Unequal Development* concerning peripheral social formations: roughly dualistic, articulationist, and tendentially unitary.[85] Generally, Bernstein characterizes Amin's major theoretical texts as 'an encyclopaedic tangle of categories and method which is self-reinforcing and results in a series of mutually contradictory propositions.'[86]

This criticism, while in my view overstated, does point to a real difficulty. Brewer rightly describes Amin's essential role, notwithstanding his original contribution, as a *synthesizer* in his field: in itself nonetheless 'an essential original contribution', but one that leads to '. . . corresponding weaknesses. On many issues, Amin tries to reconcile ideas that are in fact irreconcilable.'[87]

That this is so, is apparent even from Amin's method of work, which I would characterize as *accretive*. (Dare one say 'piecemeal accumulation', *a la* Karl Popper?) Although it would seem to be a long way (as I hope to have shown) from the empirical early works to *Class and Nation*, Amin offers little more than hints[88] as to any actual change in his *views* as distinct from his *level* of work. There is no suggestion of an 'epistemological break' between the early and late Amin. Yet, neither is his *oeuvre* a seamless web, gradually unfolding. The fact is that Amin rather eclectically (not a term of abuse in my view) has done constant 'running repairs' to his model over time. A new theme or a new debate (for example, the 'articulation of modes of production' school of P.P. Rey[89] and others) is grafted on and more or less assimilated. Even so crucial a concept for Amin as 'peripheral capitalism' can be seen, textually, thus to have crept in.[90]

Does this matter? Yes, at some level. Concrete instances of contradiction obviously demand to be resolved, and the onus is on Amin to do this. But does this strike fundamentally at Amin's whole edifice? Whether this is deemed to be so will depend, at least in part, on the critic's own theoretical persuasion.

Here issues of logic debouch into those of method. For Bernstein, who adopts Hirst's (then) essentially Althusserian approach to theory, it suffices to dub Amin's 'general characteristics of peripheral formations' as 'empirical generalizations (and of a low order)'.[91] Others less ascetic, even while accepting this at least in part, may still find considerable heuristic and empirical value in such generalizations; find them 'richer', in fact, than the actual results produced by the purveyors of 'correct' theory.[92] To be clear: I am not saying that Amin should not be brought to book (like anyone else) to explain himself. But I am saying that a bankruptcy order seems premature.

From a rather different perspective (partially based in a later-model Hirst *et al*, than that used by Bernstein)[93] Sheila Smith has drawn no less sweeping conclusions. Her criticism of Amin is in some ways that he is *too* Marxist, at least in the sense that he propounds 'a fully elaborated theoretical scheme'[94] of a kind which the new Cutlery (so unlike the not so old) deems inadmissible *per se*. Conversely, Smith praises as 'a wealth of illustrative material which is scholarly and useful'[95] precisely those parts of Amin's work which Bernstein dismisses as 'crudely inductivist'.[96]

In other respects their substantive criticisms are closer. Smith and Bernstein both fasten on Amin's 'assertion of central capitalism as a "standard" and peripheral capitalism as a "distortion"';[97] not an occasion of any difficulty for the present writer, it must be said. (Although Bernstein is right to observe that Amin says two little about 'central' formations, and what he does say may be over-general and in part wrong.)[98] Smith's more general point is that Amin so constructs his theoretical schema that there are 'built-in immunities'. For instance, 'tendencies' are specified in the model; but if these fail to show up in reality, Amin appeals to the 'dialectic'. As a result 'Amin's analysis is tautological, uninformative and sterile'.[99]

So Amin displeases Bernstein because his statements are '*not* theoretically specified', while Smith finds him 'uninformative because the basis for selection of the information *is* given by the theory'.[100] Critics are hard to please. I would not claim that Amin's conceptualization (in *The Law of Value and Historical Materialism*) of 'objective' and 'subjective' forces, economic laws and class struggle as dialectically interacting,[101] is better than anyone else's in confronting this classic methodological problem intrinsic to all social science. But I am not convinced that what the critics propose — Bernstein's theoreticist rigour, or Smith's ultimate empiricist scepticism — is better.

On one matter of *substance*, I believe Smith to be quite simply wrong about Amin. Again taking a theme from Cutler *et al*, who stress the importance of analyses at the level of the national economy,[102] she accuses Amin of ignoring this level; nay more, of ruling it out *a priori*. Evidently Smith is simply unaware of Amin's earlier work; else it would be gratuitous — not to say grotesque — to inform him of all people that 'analysis of particular national economies is an important area of work, *despite Amin's denial*'.[103]

But what she is getting at, is that Amin's more global analysis *pre-empts* economic and political initiatives at the national level. Again, considering that Amin's constant refrain — from his earliest monographs, right up to the present volume — has been to propose *concrete* strategies for *concrete* countries (or groups of countries; but the logical point is the same), this criticism seems altogether misplaced. And, once again, it is hard to please everyone; for inasmuch as Amin *does* enter into the terrain of the national economy, he is at once pounced upon by those other critics who have dubbed him an ideologist of the national bourgeoisie!

Or the *same* critics, even. For the trenchant dismissal (quoted earlier) of Amin as 'nationalistic, simplistic',[104] was also by Smith, who appears to want to have it both ways. After all, the 'break with the world capitalist system', which Amin is held to advocate, is nothing if not a project at the level of the national economy! 'Dangerous arrogance' is Smith's (somewhat unspecified) judgement on the idea of the 'break'.[105] I have argued elsewhere that it *is* possible (and indeed unavoidable) to specify a theory of 'national self-reliance' as a Marxist project.[106] Admittedly, Amin scarcely does this in any detail; but there are other examples, both in theory (for example, Senghaas, Thomas) and practice (North Korea notably, but also China, Albania, and others).[106]

And Pol Pot? I do not know what Amin's position on the Khmer Rouge *debacle* is now. His short article on 'The Lesson of Cambodia', dating from 1976, retains its interest as a political sociology of how the revolution was made.[108] But the type of economy, polity and society subsequently 'built' (if that is the word) so bloodily by the Khmer Rouge, has not the slightest connection with the kind of regionally based, interacting, and above all *industrializing* self-reliance favoured by Amin — and practised in what are the real test-cases of the 'autocentric' path, notably North Korea.[109]

Any dependency theorist has to face up to Pol Pot, just as (no more and no less) any Marxist has to face up to Stalin. Both of these horrors of our century require the most honest and rigorous thought. Yet, at the end of the day, in neither case, do I believe that the general project is gainsaid by its horrendous exemplar. Amin does not deserve this 'guilt by association'.

The claim that Samir Amin's theories simply do not fit the facts is on a different level altogether. An article by Schiffer offers a mountain of statistical evidence about post-war development trends, which, in his view, simply controvert Amin's theses in almost every particular.[110] Clearly this demands more detailed consideration than is possible here, but some general comments may be ventured.

Schiffer's position is basically Warrenite: the 'facts' (that is, the figures) show that 'the post-war performance of the LDCs [less developed countries] has been extremely impressive.'[111] Everything hinges, no doubt, on the *interpretation* of the facts. Nothing in Amin's model denies the possibility of rapid quantitative growth, in terms of the usual indicators (one has only to recall his study of the Ivory Coast). Even so, the countries on whose performance Schiffer focuses are often the notable 'heavyweights' of the Third World (cf. especially his Tables 1, 2 and 6).[112] Equally notable, for an article about Samir Amin, is the relative lack of specific consideration of Africa in the tables (e.g. Tables 3, 5 and 10).[113]

Obviously, much hinges on the choice of indices. What would trends in *unemployment* show, for example, alongside Schiffer's vaunted increases in employment? As long as the latter's overall rate of increase fails to keep pace with population growth,[114] then *both* employment and unemployment may rise. In other instances, one wonders about the relation between percentage and absolute magnitudes. Thus, Table 2 suggests that LDCs now have higher rates of saving than developed countries, and further that this is generated *'overwhelmingly from local resources'*. (Even multi-national corporations, adds Schiffer insouciantly, are 'safely' tapping *local* capital markets rather than — as Amin would have it — importing fresh capital.[115] But origins aside, is the *rate* of saving so crucial as the *amount*? Is either adequate, quantitatively or qualitatively, to *transform* these economies? Amin is talking about transformation, not growth.

One issue where it can be granted that Schiffer does confront Amin on his own ground is the question of the domestic market: its presence or absence, its dynamic potential, its composition as between 'luxury' or 'mass consumption' goods. Schiffer rejects the latter distinction of Amin's, even though he finds a relationship between the growth of the capital goods sector and the production of consumer durables which precisely matches Amin's model.[116] The key evidence here is in Table 4, where Schiffer claims (via a complex process of deduction and subtraction) that much the largest component of total value added is 'attributable' to consumer non-durables. Nor, he adds, should this surprise any Marxist.[117] Yet this is not the same as *directly* investigating the structure of the home mass market, difficult though this is.

Nonetheless, it has to be said that other dependency theorists (notably Cardoso)[118] do not base their theories, as does Amin, on the alleged impossibility of such a market, which, indeed, is plausibly claimed to exist in Brazil and elsewhere. In some sense, obviously, there is always a domestic 'mass' market: short of absolute subsistence, the masses have some money and they spend it on some things. This must be studied concretely. But the interesting questions about the type, composition, and dynamizing potential of this market only begin here. Data such as Schiffer's are suggestive, but on their own they can tell us little one way or the other about the *distortions* in structures of production and consumption which are Amin's concern. Schiffer could hardly raise such questions, since he appears to operate with a unilinear and quantitative model of capitalist progress (like Warren); thus automatically entailing that everything in the garden is lovely, provided the growth rates keep up.

Perhaps the last word in criticism of Amin[119] may go to a trio of commentators, who describe his model as at once composed of 'platitudes' and 'far-fetched'. They, too, criticize as a 'reactionary utopia' his call for a break with the world market, as also his advice that the rules of profitability should be rejected in the allocation of resources. *Contra* Amin, planning is allegedly possible even in a dependent country. Increasing exports should not be rejected. Doubtless it will do nothing to weaken Amin's present rather frantic excoriations of the unholy alliances of revisionist Marxism, social democracy, Trotskyism, etc., etc. ('Northern Marxism', might one suggest?) to reveal that the authors of these criticisms are Soviet scholars.[120]

Conclusion

I hope that the foregoing has succeeded in giving some impression of the range and scale of Samir Amin's work. It will be evident that I view it, not as a closed system or a rigorous theory (although it certainly contains rigorous theories), but more as a Herculean attempt to confront the many-faceted and rapidly changing phenomenon of underdevelopment in our day — in general and in its specificities; in theory, and in practice.

Samir Amin is barely 50; his work is by no means at an end. Where does he go from here? It is in this connection that the present work is intriguing. Slight as it is, it appears to mark a double return for Amin: to empirical work, and to his earliest roots (personal, political, and academic) in the Arab world.

Essentially, Amin here offers a quantitative analysis with a message, hence a project. He aims to show how the countries of the Arab world *could*, with their heterogeneous resources and revenues, combine to form a '*grand espace*', an integrated and dynamic economic unit. Thus would the oil revenues benefit future generations, rather than simply revert to the financial centres and hence, industries, of the West.

Although questions could be raised about the present work — its brevity, its indices, and particular points etc., etc., — the *direction* which it suggests for Amin's work seems promising. Yet it is only a beginning and a small one at that (contrast it with his 500 pages of intricate detail on the Maghreb of 15 years ago!). Is it too much to hope that he might expand this into a fuller and more closely argued study, offering the kind of painstaking detail combined with structural analysis which his work of the 1960s achieved so well? 'Back to the concrete' seems to be the rallying cry of the moment. Certainly, it is hard to imagine how further progress at the level of totalizing theory can be made, at least for a while.

Meanwhile, for an assessment of Amin's accomplishment to date, one cannot do better than to quote that most painstaking and fairest of critics (not only of Amin), Anthony Brewer:

> [Amin's] is the only serious attempt to tackle what is surely the central problem, that of analysing accumulation on a world scale, a dynamic process involving social formations of very divergent structures linked into a single world capitalist economy. In the process, he has tried to link together a range of subjects that had previously been studied in virtual isolation from each other: modes of production, class structures in the periphery, the pattern of international trade and specialisation, the formation of international prices, the (economic) problems of national development in the periphery, the periodisation of capitalist development and so on. To pose the problem is often the most important step.[121]

That the questions which Amin has raised (and, in at least some cases, gone a long way towards answering) *are* real questions, and are *the* questions, has been the premise of this paper. It is to be hoped that future work will go forward on this basis, the basis which Amin has done so much to illuminate. Above all, I hope there will be no widespread or lasting retreat into a Eurocentric Marxism disguised as universalism, twinned with a 'Socialism' whose practical message to the Third World would appear to be an undifferentiated paean of praise for capitalism.[122]

Quite possibly, in the Third World as once in Europe, the staying power and transformative capacity of capitalism have been underestimated. In this case, I doubt whether Amin will ignore the principle which he eloquently expressed in the afterword to *Accumulation on a World Scale:*

> History did not come to a halt in 1880, nor in 1917, nor in 1945. In each decade, new facts appear which indicate new developments *unsuspected at previous stages.* History is no more unilinear today than it was five centuries ago . . . . Uneven development remains the only rule, and it always confounds the would-be prophets. Besides, the outcome of political struggles determines at each moment new alternatives which are both unforseen and unforseeable. So it is necessary at each stage to take seriously the task of integrating new facts into the analysis. This appears quite obvious. And yet there will always be individuals searching for absolute certainties who will refuse to do this, thereby being forced either to ignore the facts or to try and squeeze them at all costs into a scheme which did not anticipate them . . .
>
> They prefer the reassuring religious vision of apocalyptic catastrophe and a golden age miraculously created at a single stroke, instead of the disturbing prospect of perpetually changing conditions which necessitate continuous rethinking.[123]

Notes

1. See Section III below, 'Amin and his critics'.
2. Notably in the case of Amin's collected essays; see n.7 below.
3. B.9 (e), B.10 (e). (See Bibliography for key to abbreviations used for the titles of Amin's works).
4. B.6

5. B.4
6. B.7.
7. B.14(e), B.15. For further details on these, see my review of both volumes: Foster-Carter (X.15).
8. See B.14(e), esp. chs. 3, 4, 7, 9, 10; also 74.10.
9. T.1 (1955).
10. T.2 (1957).
11. B.11, p.1; also p.303, n.1.
12. B.11(e), p.1.
13. B.11(e), p.303, n.1.
14. *Ibid.*
15. 55.01.
16. See e.g. 56.02, 60.02, 62.03, 70.03, 70.05.
17. 55.01, 56.01, 58.01, 58.02, 59.01, 60.01, 60.02, 60.03, 61.01, 62.03, 63.01.
18. See especially 58.01, which is in fact a series of seven such papers.
19. See Olivier (X.9.a), and the discussion in Section III below.
20. B.1.
21. B.2.
22. B.3.
23. B.4.
24. B.5. (Interestingly, this book seems to have appeared a year *earlier* in its Polish translation).
25. B.9(e).
26. B.6.
27. T.3.
28. B.7.
29. B.8.
30. B.10(e). The choice of English title is all the more perverse, inasmuch as Amin has said that he regards the term 'neo-colonialism' as 'unscientific'. (B.15, p.32, n.9).
31. B.19(e).
32. B.10(e), p.236.
33. See, for Latin America, e.g. Dos Santos (1973).
34. Frank (1967), and subsequent works.
35. Thomas (1974).
36. B.6., back page.
37. Other West African states receive cursory reference in the Introduction (pp. xv-xvii).
38. Fanon (1967).
39. See also Amin's two summary articles on aspects of the Senegalese business class: 69.02, and 71.06.
40. See the controversy between Kaplinsky, Leys, and others in *Rev. Af. Pol. Econ.* (1980).
41. Above all, Warren (1980).
42. B.15.
43. 67.01.
44. 71.09.
45. 74.02.
46. 69.01, 70.02, 72.04, 72.05, 73.01, 75.05.

47. 67.02, 72.01.
48. B.11(e), pp.364-77; B.12(e), pp.317-32.
49. 70.07.
50. 63.02.
51. 63.02, e.2, pp.42-3.
52. See pp.80-1 of this book.
53. Brewer, (X.2.a), p. 233.
54. B.11(e), p.2.
55. *Ibid.*, ch.3.
56. 74.15.
57. Cheng, (X.4), pp. 59-60.
58. Emmanuel (1972).
59. 72.02.
60. 13(e), 14(e).
61. See e.g. 14(e), Introduction, pp.6-7. Debates which Amin here declares 'appear closed, at least provisionally' include: ideology — infrastructure relations in pre-capitalist modes of production; alienation; the 'transformation' of values into prices; and 'the discussions of underdevelopment' *tout court.*
62. 14(e), chs. 1,2,6; cf. 74.01, 74.03, 75.04.
63. Brewer, *op cit.* pp. 243-50; see also his chapter 9, on Emmanuel.
64. 18(e).
65. B.12(e), pp.13-16.
66. B.19(e), p.X.
67. B.12(e), p.383; B.19(e), p.17.
68. E.g. B.18(e), p.122 ff.
69. *Ibid*, p.108, pp.118-9 and ff.
70. B.19(e), p.149 ff (esp. table 1, p.151).
71. E.g. Smith, (X.14.b).
72. See the passage from B.11(e) quoted at the end of this Introduction.
73. B.16(e). See the interesting review of this by Ja 'far (X.7).
74. B.16(e), pp. 113-4.
75. This point is argued in a forthcoming paper: 'Conceptualizing Nations: a problem in Marxism revisited'.
76. B.14(e), chs 9.10,7;4,3; cf. also 78.02, and many of Amin's articles over the last five years or so.
77. See especially B.17(e); 74.13.
78. E.g. B.18(e), pp.117-122, in which our hero lays about him at a motley host of dragons, including: the Soviet Academy, Perry Anderson, 'Western Marxism', Geoffrey Kay ('Marxism *a la* Cecil Rhodes'), unspecified 'American radical' writers on M.N.Cs,, Palloix, 'the Trotskyist cohort and the revisionist and semirevisionist academicians', ethnography (especially Sahlins), Tokei, Godelier, and the *nouveaux philosophis!.*'
79. Olivier, (X.9.a).
80. Amin, (X.9.b; 75.11). See also Olivier's last word, *ibid* (X.9.c).
81. Smith, (X.14.b).
82. *Ibid.*
83. Brewer, (X.2.b).
84. *Ibid*, p.115.

85. Bernstein, (X.1), p.88.
86. *Ibid*, p.98.
87. Brewer, (X.2.a), p. 233.
88. E.g. in 19(e), p.vii.
89. Rey, (1973).
90. Compare these two formulations, which conclude passages otherwise identical: (a) '. . . not the general difficulties characteristic of capitalist development, but those peculiar to *a late development in the context of a world where capitalism is dominant.*' (B.15, p.94; 1967 version). (b) (The same, except) '. . . those peculiar to *the development of peripheral capitalism*'. B.11(e), p. 377; 1970 version. (My emphasis, in both instances)..
91. Bernstein, *op. cit.*, p.89.
92. For such an argument in favour of the richness of neo-Marxist writing more generally, even if its theoretical shoelaces are sometimes undone, see Mouzelis (1980), p.369.
93. Cutler, Hindess, Hirst and Hussain (1977).
94. Smith, (X.14.a), p.5.
95. *Ibid*, p.9.
96. Bernstein, *op. cit.*, p.89.
97. Smith, (X.14.a), pp.13, 14-15.
98. Bernstein, *op. cit.*, p.91. The analysis of 'central' formations in underdevelopment theory is a nettle which few have grasped; but see Senghaas and Menzel (1980).
99. Smith (X.14.a), pp.12-13.
100. Bernstein, *op. cit.*, p.89; Smith (X.14.a), p.13. (My emphasis).
101. B.18(e), e.g. ch.2 pp.31-5, and *passim.*
102. Cutler *et. al.*, *op. cit.*, e.g. pp.243-54 of Vol.2.
103. Smith, (X.14.a), pp.18-19.
104. Smith, (X.14.b).
105. Smith, (X.14.a), p.20.
106. Foster-Carter, n.d.
107. See Thomas (1974), *op. cit.*, Senghaas (1981), on North Korea, Foster-Carter (1977); on other countries, works produced as part of the research project guided by Senghaas, and cited in his (1981).
108. B.14(e).
109. I discuss further the difference between Pol Pot's Kampuchea and genuine examples of autocentric development in Foster-Carter, n.d.
110. Schiffer (X.13), p.532.
111. *Ibid.*, p.518.
112. *Ibid*, p.519,520,529.
113. *Ibid*, p.522,528,532.
114. As is indeed the case; cf. Schiffer's tables, p.530.
115. *Ibid*, p.520 (original emphasis), 521.
116. *Ibid.* p.528.
117. *Ibid*, pp.523-7.
118. I have heard Cardoso stress this as a major point of difference with Amin and others.

119. Shortage of space precludes detailed consideration of other critiques of Amin; e.g. Leaver's interesting if somewhat idiosyncratic attempt to 'situate' him. Leaver (X.8.)
120. Rubinstein *et. al.* (X.12), pp.104,105-6,107-8.
121. Brewer (X.2.a), p.257.
122. This seems to me to be the unfortunate effect of 'Warrenism'; *cf.* Warren (1980).
123. B.11(e), p.590, emphasis in original. (I have chosen to retain my own translation, made before the English edition had appeared, only because I happen to prefer it on minor stylistic grounds to Brian Pearce's — here, as always — undoubtedly excellent rendition).

Works Cited in Introduction

(other than works by Amin, and by those who debate his ideas; these are listed separately, in the main Bibliography).

Dos Santos, Teotonio, 'The Crisis of Development Theory and the Problem of Dependence in Latin America' in Bernstein, Henry (ed.) *Underdevelopment and Development* (Harmondsworth, Penguin, 1973).

Emmanuel, Arghiri, *Unequal Exchange* (London, New Left Books, 1972).

Fanon, Frantz, *The Wretched of the Earth* (Harmondsworth, Penguin, 1967).

Cutler A., Hindess, B., Hirst, P., Hussain, A., *Marx's Capital and Capitalism Today* (2 vols), (London, Routledge & Kegan Paul, 1977, 1978).

Foster-Carter, Aidan, (n.d.). "National Self-Reliance" as a project in Marxism'. In *Idem* & Gurnah, Ahmed (eds.), *Explanation and Action in Marxist Theory* (forthcoming).

Foster -Carter, Aidan, 'North Korea: Development and Self-Reliance — A Critical Appraisal'. In: Gittings, John and MacCormack, Gavan (eds.) *Crisis in Korea* (Nottingham, Spokesman, 1977).

Frank, Andre Gunder, *Capitalism and Underdevelopment in Latin America* (New York, Monthly Review Press, 1967).

Kaplinsky, Raphael, *et. al.* 'Debate on "Dependency" in Kenya'. *Review of African Political Economy* No.17 (Jan-April 1980) pp. 83-113.

Mouzelis, Nicos, 'Modernization, Underdevelopment, Uneven Development', *J. Peasant Studies*, 7:3, April 1980.

Rey, Pierre-Philippe, *Les Alliances de Classes* (Paris, Maspero, 1973).

Senghaas, Dieter, 'Socialism in Historical and Developmental Perspective' *Economics* (Tubingen), vol.23, 1981, pp.94-115.

Senghaas, Dieter and Menzel, Ulrich, 'Autocentric Development Despite International Competence Differentials' *Economics* (Tubingen), vol.21. 1980,pp.7-35.

Thomas, Clive Y., *Dependence and Transformation* (New York, Monthly Review Press, 1974).

Warren, Bill, *Imperialism: Pioneer of Capitalism* (London, New Left Books, 1980).

1. Can One Speak of an Arab Economy?

The Arab world today is neither a political nor an economic unit. Each of the Arab states is integrated as a separate unit into the world capitalist system. The historical foundations, modalities and extent of this integration are particular to each country and constitute objective factors which militate against the economic unity of the Arab world. Having achieved independence on the basis of state frontiers which were largely the results of recent history, the Arab states have each evolved in their own way; the organized political forces operating within the individual context of these states have moved towards specific and often divergent orientations. Differences over frontiers or about regional hegemony have repeatedly been a source of dispute and opposition amongst them.

Under such conditions, one cannot really speak of an Arab economy *per se*. One can at most speak of the economy of the Arab region as a particular constellation of Third World states. It is, in fact, a particularly heterogeneous sample. The populations of the different Arab states range from less than 100,000 inhabitants to 40 million; their annual per capita income varies from $100 to $15,000; their level of industrial development runs from zero to that of the most advanced 'semi-industrialized' Third World states; their degree of state organization and the extent of their public service provision (notably in education), as measured by the volume of public expenditure, includes some of the lowest in the Third World (10% of Gross Domestic Product (G.D.P.)), as well as some of the highest (30% of G.D.P.); finally, their level of integration into the international division of labour, as measured by the proportion of the G.D.P. accounted for by exports, stretches from 3% to 81%.

We have, none the less, chosen to speak in terms of an Arab economy, primarily for political reasons. The decision to move towards Arab unity is probably an historical necessity and may well become a concrete possibility in the foreseeable future. The decision has firm historical foundations which have already produced lasting effects. All Arab political forces have to situate themselves in terms of this option, and strong unifying currents do sweep through the entire region.

Even at the most banal level of economic interaction, the effects of this tendency towards unity can be felt. Granted, inter-Arab trade remains negligible. Arab economic policies and five-year plans are based on a competitive rather than mutually complementary strategy, notably in industry. It is also true that the fiscal systems of the Arab world are still too different from one another to promote substantial trade and that the prevailing monetary systems remain autonomous, despite the existence of an Arab monetary fund, whose activities are restricted to backing International Monetary Fund (I.M.F.) interventions in the area. And admittedly, the attempted 'unions' (Maghreb, Arab Common Market, etc.) are more akin to declarations of intent than to even the most marginal of real achievements, when they are not simply forgotten altogether in the tumult of regional conflicts. Yet in two essential domains, namely the movement of private and public capital (by the various states and national or Pan-Arab banks and funds) and the movements of the labour force, there is already a marked tendency to make co-operative use of the various factors of production. Transcending short-term vicissitudes, this tendency will continue to develop, as it has for the past 20 years, most noticeably during the 1970s which saw a considerable acceleration. The new situation which results is likely to call for extensive revisions of national policies.

The Four Main Groups of Arab Countries:
Four main groups of countries can be distinguished within the diversity of the Arab world:

Group A: We can designate Libya, Saudi Arabia, Kuwait, Qatar, Bahrain, the Emirates and Oman as all of them oil-rich countries where the small size of the population and the lack of any other important resource mean that oil accounts for most economic activity and shapes almost every aspect of economic life.

Group B: This second group comprises only Algeria and Iraq. In their case, oil revenues act upon more complex societies whose development is, in many ways, accelerated as a result.

Group C: The third group comprises the semi-industrialized Arab countries with no oil: Morocco, Tunisia, Egypt, Lebanon and Syria.

Group D: Finally, we have the least advanced and least industrialized countries: Mauritania, Sudan, Yemen, Democratic Yemen, Somalia and Djibouti. Because of their particular situation, Jordan and occupied Palestine can also be placed in this group.

The Group A countries account for only 10% of the Arab population, but they concentrate within themselves about half of the total Arab G.D.P. (representing some $6,000 per capita) and provide 55% of the region's exports. Although only a small proportion of the population is employed in the oil sector itself, oil revenues orient every aspect of economic and social policy and also generate a large surplus which is held abroad. Oil represents about half of the G.D.P., agriculture is negligible in these desert regions, and industry is only just starting up. Thus, apart from oil, services and the state sector, whose income is in any case largely drawn from oil revenues, remain the only force for change.

The Group B countries represent about 20% of the population of the Arab world and account for a more or less equivalent proportion of its total G.D.P. (roughly $1,000 per capita). Exports represent 45% of the G.D.P. (the average for the Arab world is 60%). Agriculture is a weak sector in this group, as in the whole Arab world (8% of the group's G.D.P., as against 9% overall), but is still significant, both in actual production and in its potential for the future. The relatively recently established industrial base of these countries has progressed rapidly, enabling them to catch up with or even overtake many countries which had made a head start in industrialization. The group's industry accounts for 15% of its G.D.P. (Arab average: 7.2%). On average, the Group B countries are in many ways similar to what a united Arab world might look like.

The Group C countries account for the majority of the Arab population — more than 51% — but for only 20% of its G.D.P. (per capita income: $500). The economies of the countries in this group are more diversified and industry has been established longer. Agriculture provides 23% of the G.D.P., as against industry's 14%. The level of exports is relatively modest: 20% of G.D.P. None the less, these countries, notably Egypt, form a substantial whole, accounting for 56% of Arab agricultural production and 42% of Arab industrial production. Thus, the Group C countries strongly resemble the Arab world as a whole in the days before the oil boom of the 1970s.

The Group D countries are particularly underprivileged. The data concerning them are the least precise but one can estimate that per capita income does not exceed $300, largely provided by agriculture (roughly 40%), while industry plays a negligible role (less than 5% of G.D.P.).

Taking the Arab world as a whole, one is struck by the scale and prevailing direction of movement of the factors of production.

The foreign trade of the A and B groups accounts for 90% of the overall volume of the Arab world's exports, but for only 70% of its imports. By contrast, the C and D groups' imports considerably exceed their exports. However, the trade surplus of the first group (about $50 billion, 30% of Arab G.D.P.) is far greater than the second group's deficit ($5 billion, or about 3% of Arab G.D.P. and 9% of the second group's G.D.P.). The bulk of the Arab surplus is not held in the Arab world itself, and the deficit countries receive aid and capital inflows from other countries. But the fact remains that the flow of capital from the first group (and especially Group A) to the second, fulfils a range of decisive economic and political functions; it attenuates the explosive contradictions of Group C.

The economic situation of the Arab countries which make up Group C is quite simply bad. Having opted for a form of development which is profoundly integrated into the world division of labour, but lacking the means to pursue this development because of the shortfall in their exportable production, these countries are finding it very difficult to maintain growth. Egypt and Syria at one stage responded to these constraints by implementing radical reforms (land reform and nationalization). Others have followed a similar course, but more slowly (Tunisia), or even in some cases so slowly as not to enter into any conflict with the pre-existing political systems (Morocco).

There is a great difference between the situations of Group C and Group B (Iraq and Algeria). Group B is implementing a development strategy which is not notably different from that attempted by the Group C countries, particularly during the 1960s. But the Group B countries can actually afford this course, thanks to their oil exports. Thus, although the difficulties the B Group is already encountering, and will no doubt continue to run into, are not essentially different from those met by the C Group, there is, none the less, a clear contrast between the two types of growth, at least in the present and for the immediate future.

As for the D Group, it remains relatively stable in its poverty. Its structures have in fact been relatively undisturbed by integration into the world capitalist market and it therefore has far more modest needs in terms of reproducing its present equilibrium. The very slow rhythm of development in these countries reflects this situation.

The movement of labour is exactly the opposite to that of capital: it flows from the C Group to the A Group. Egypt is the main exporter of labour: about two million people have left to work in the Gulf and in Libya. Tunisia also provides Libya with a substantial workforce. For obvious political reasons, Palestine is the third largest supplier of labour in absolute terms, and the first in relative terms. Other regions of the Arab world have been and continue to be important sources of emigrants, but towards Europe not towards the Arab world. This has long been the case in the Maghreb and, more recently, in Lebanon. Finally, North Yemen is traditionally a source of migrant labour for the Gulf countries. Furthermore, the Gulf countries also draw on non-Arab immigrant labour, notably from Pakistan.

The movement of labour fulfils a double function. On the one hand, it attenuates the contradictions within the C Group, where the wages sent home by the emigrants augment the inflow of capital. On the other hand, it is a key factor in the economic growth of the A Group countries.

One decisive economic and political fact emerges from all this; limited as it may be in purely quantitative terms, the movement of the factors of production strengthens the links within the Arab world and plays an essential role in the reproduction of its equilibrium. To the extent that one can envisage the gradual development of an overall strategy, this movement could become a powerful force for integration and unity.

Tables 1 to 4 in the Statistical Appendix illustrate the elements on which we have based this analysis. They were drawn up from data which was gathered under conditions which did not always guarantee access to the most reliable sources; none the less, we believe they are sufficiently correct to illustrate the point. They embrace all the member countries of the Arab League, with the exception of Somalia and Djibouti (the inclusion of these two countries, whose population in 1976 was 3,280,000 and whose G.D.P. was $753 million would not modify the overall results), and they also include data from Egypt, although this country is not at present a member of the League.

The Tables 1 to 4 illustrate various points:

(a) The relative weight acquired by the Gulf countries, notably Saudi Arabia, since 1973, and correspondingly, the role of oil exports and the oil surplus. Saudi Arabia alone accounts for 25% of Arab G.D.P.

(b) The divergent evolution of Morocco (and to a lesser degree, of Tunisia) compared to Algeria. Starting from a position of rough equality in the early 1960s, Algeria's G.D.P. is now double that of Morocco's, its industrial base is 75% larger, its per capita consumption 35% higher, its gross investment 3.6 times greater and its government expenditure 80% more. Clearly the two countries' rates of growth in the period 1965—76 were very different. The same divergence is noticeable between Iraq and Syria: since then, Iraq has had a steady four points lead in annual per capita growth and its per capita G.D.P. is now 75% greater than Syria's.

(c) The unfavourable position of Egypt, whose G.D.P. is now of the same order of magnitude as Libya's, Algeria's or Iraq's. However, Egypt remains the biggest agricultural producer ($4.5 billion, as against Morocco's $1.9 billion, in second place) and retains its lead in industry ($2.5 billion, as against Algeria's $2.1 billion).

(d) The intense disparities in investment, correlated to the respective growth rates. The average rate for the A and B countries is around 26% of G.D.P., as against 17% for the C and D groups.

(e) The poor performance of agricultural production and the modest scale of industrial development. Apart from oil, Arab production is of the order of $80 billion. The rural economy, which employs 56% of the population, supplies $15 billion worth of products, representing 18% of the relevant total. The urban economy's $65 billion (82%) is due less to industry ($11.6 billion, 18% of the urban economy's production) than to services in the broad sense. As we shall see later, the structure of industry remains rudimentary.

2. The Arab Economy and the World Capitalist System

The Arab world occupies a very special place within the Third World, of which it is the region most fully integrated into the contemporary world system.

This fact certainly has deep-rooted historical origins. The Arab world has always maintained some association with Europe. Until the end of the Middle Ages, the two worlds were comparable in terms of their stage and level of development; indeed, in many domains, the Arabs often held the lead. The gap began to grow during the mercantilist era from the 15th to the 18th Centuries. The Arab world was quick to react to this challenge, especially Egypt, from the early 19th Century onwards. We have dealt elsewhere with the causes and effects of this divergent evolution (Cf. S. Amin, *The Arab Nation*). As a result, the Arab world was integrated into the world capitalist system, as a dominated periphery, at an earlier stage than the other regions of the Third World, with the obvious exception of Latin America and the Caribbean. It is thus not surprising that it should at present be more fully integrated into the world system than Black Africa, South and South East Asia, or Eastern Asia.

The modalities of this integration were, however, by no means homogeneous. In North Africa, French colonization, starting early in the 19th Century in Algeria, threatened the region as a whole with the kind of settler colonization corresponding to a relatively unevolved stage of capitalist development in the metropole. The same pattern was nearly reproduced with the Italian colonization of Libya. Egypt had already been considerably integrated into the international division of labour since the era of Mohammed Ali and the Khedives, even before the British occupation. By contrast, the countries of the Fertile Crescent were only very slightly integrated into this international division of labour throughout the Ottoman period. As for the Gulf countries, their integration, which was concomitant with the growth of the oil industry, goes back little further than the end of the Second World War, while North Yemen and Oman are still later arrivals. The political and cultural as well as economic effects of these various forms of integration are examined in *The Arab Nation*, to which we refer the reader.

A first indicator of the extent of participation in the international division of labour is naturally provided by the ratio of exports (and/or imports) to G.D.P. This index is much higher for the Arab world than for any other region of the Third World. The ratio of exports to G.D.P. is now of the order of 60% for the Arab world, as against 22% for Sub-saharan Africa, 14% for South, South East and East Asia (excluding China and Japan), and 13% for Latin America and the Caribbean. Even before the 1973-74 hike in oil prices, the Arab percentage was around 30%. As for the ratio between imports and G.D.P., it can be estimated at around 32% for the Arab world, as against 22% for Africa, 16% for Asia and 14% for Latin America and the Caribbean. Before 1970, the ratio for the Arab world was already around 28%.

There are probably several countries, notably big oil producers such as Venezuela or rich mining countries such as Gabon and Zaire, which would display indices similar to those characteristic of the Arab world. But no *region* with so large a population — something like 150 million inhabitants — presents so high a level of integration. The exceptional importance of Arab imports relative to the volume of agricultural and industrial production and investment expresses the particularly high level of interpenetration of the economies of the Arab world and the developed world, both in terms of the structure of the model of development and with regard to the organization of the productive process.

Excluding oil production, Arab agricultural production represents 18% of the region's total output, compared to 32%

Varying Degrees of Third World Reliance on Imports, by Region (%)

	Agricultural Production as % of G.D.P.	*Industrial Production as % of G.D.P.*	*Fixed Gross Capital Formation as % of G.D.P.*	*1+2+3 as % of G.D.P.*	*Imports as % of G.D.P.*	*5/4*	*Col. 6 expressed as an Index*
Arab World (excluding oil)	18	15	36	69	51	74	100
Black Africa	32	11	17	60	22	37	50
South, South East and East Asia (excluding China and Japan)	40	15	17	72	16	22	30
Latin America and Caribbean	13	24	20	57	14	25	34

for Africa, 40% for Asia and 13% for Latin America. The equivalent percentages for industry are 15% in the Arab world, 11% in Africa, 15% in Asia and 24% in Latin America. As for the volume of gross investment, it is equivalent to 36% of the Arab region's production (excluding oil), as against 17% in Africa and Asia and 20% for Latin America.

Thus, if one relates the volume of imports to that of agricultural production, industrial production and capital formation taken together, it emerges that the role of imports in consumption and production is much greater in the Arab world than in any other region of the Third World, as can be seen from the table on p. 50.

The implications of this data can be summed up as follows: the contribution of imports to consumption and investment in the Arab world is twice as important as in Black Africa, three times more important than in Latin America and the Caribbean, 3.3 times more important than in South and East Asia. In other words, the Arab economy is more externally oriented — and hence more dependent — than the economies of the rest of the Third World.

A more precise examination of the structure of consumption, inter-industrial exchange and imports will enable us to elaborate on this conclusion.

3. Consumption and Production Structures

Tables 5 to 11 in the Statistical Appendix enable us to analyse the structures of Arab consumption and the Arab system of production in some depth.

We set out to establish a complete picture of inter-industrial relations within the Arab world as a whole. Table 11 covers eleven sectors of economic activity: (1) agriculture, (2) mining, energy and oil, (3) agricultural processing and food industries, (4) other light industries (textiles, leather, timber), (5) chemicals, (6) building materials, (7) metals and engineering, (8) construction and public works, (9) transport and communications, (10) trade, (11) assorted services (public and private).

An analysis of the composition of imports (Table 5), based on the prevailing methods of classifying foreign trade, and incorporating a few simple hypotheses as to the distribution of various types of imports across the relevant sectors, enables us to establish the horizontal vector for imports corresponding to the intersectorial table.

The structure of exports, in which oil and oil products play a dominant role, is similarly analysed (Table 6), in order to construct the vertical vector for exports corresponding to the categories of Table 11.

The resulting vertical vectors for final demand are presented again in Table 7. The table shows, firstly, that the structure of demand relating to gross fixed capital formation, as set out in Column 7, comprises two relatively equal and stable components of investment, namely equipment (machinery and transport) supplied by Sector 7, and construction and public works provided by Sector 8. Using a series of national accounts relating to different years, we have made sure that the averages presented here do not deviate far from the relevant norms. Stock fluctuation has not been taken into account.

The second thing that Table 7 portrays is the structure of administrative expenditure (Column 6). This has also been determined in equal measure by a relatively rough but fixed division between salaries paid by public authorities on the one hand (47%), and expenditure on goods and services, attributed to Sectors 1 to 11 according to average proportions drawn from the national accounts of the main Arab countries, on the other. Once again, to simplify the presentation, we have omitted expenditure on imported armaments, for which official statistics are in any case mostly unavailable and which is usually financed through special agreements. Given this exception, the figures for administrative expenditure cover the whole range of state activity, including public services (education, health, etc.), general economic services, and administrative services (general administration, police, courts, current expenditure on the armed forces: barracks' maintenance and soldiers' pay, etc.) The state's interventions in production (subsidies and investment, subventions to the state sector and the economy as a whole, etc.) are obviously excluded from this analysis.

Thirdly, there is the vertical vector for household expenditure or consumption (shown in Column 5), which was obtained in two ways: partly from the difference between resources and employment in the intersectorial table (Table 11) and partly by the extrapolation of average ratios drawn from the national accounts of the main Arab countries. The vector obtained tallies closely with this average. We shall later take a closer look at the methods used to apportion the two components of this vector, namely consumption corresponding to the reproduction of the labour force and surplus consumption (Columns 1, 2 and 3, Table 7 and Table 8).

The square section of the intersectorial table (Table 11), corresponding to technical coefficients, was worked out in stages as follows: First, nine industrial sectors were considered (see Table 4) and regrouped into five sectors (Table 9). For each of the 11 sectors (agriculture, oil, industries, services), we considered the input of raw materials and semi-finished products provided by Sectors 1 to 7. In other words, we integrated the expenditure on building maintenance into retained gross profits (as a part of added value) allocated to finance gross investment. The two exceptions were retail outlet buildings (Sector 10) and buildings allocated to the various services (Sector 11). Transport and trade margins and service inputs were considered separately.

Table 9 thus illustrates the technical coefficients corresponding to productive consumption of inputs 1 to 7 for sectors 1 to 9, and inputs 1 to 8 for Sectors 10 and 11. These coefficients were obtained from the available detailed input-output tables for the main Arab countries. We took careful note of the coefficients relating to particular sub-sectors (for instance, steelmaking or phosphate fertilizer manufacture) and recomposed each sector so as to give each of the specific coefficients a weighting appropriate to the composition of each sector within the Arab world as a whole. The notes accompanying Table 9 outline the main principles used.

We then turned to the margins accounted for by transport, trade and services (Table 10). From our survey of the national accounts of the main Arab countries, we reached a global figure for these margins, which could be related to the sum of local production plus Imports. The accounts showed that the proportion represented by the margins relating to Sectors 3 to 7 inclusive was around an average of 20%; the figure for agriculture was lower, around 13% (given the level of peasant subsistence consumption), and it was only 3.7% for Sector 2 (electricity, mining and oil). The margins for transport, trade and services on imports were around 15% for foodstuffs, 12% for capital goods, 25% for intermediate products and 40% for consumer durables. The margins were then allocated amongst the three components (transport, trade and services) so as to match the totals representing these three sectors in the aggregate national accounts of the main countries. We then had at our disposal all the elements required to construct Table 11.

The exceptionally high level of the Arab economy's integration into the world system of international division of labour is clearly reflected in Table 11.

The proportion of imports in final household consumption of products 1 to 7 is very high, as is shown in the table here. The proportion of imports is no doubt slightly overestimated, since some imported products are consumed by governments directly. Governments consume products of Sectors 1 to 7 to a value of $9 billion. Assuming that half of these products were imported, the proportion of overall household consumption accounted for by imported products would fall from 46% to 36%. None the less, these calculations make two things quite clear.

Household Consumption: Reliance on Imports

	Household Consumption ($ billions)	*Of Which Imports ($ billions)* C.I.F.	*Market Price*	*Imports as % of Household Consumption*
Agricultural Products and Foodstuffs (Sectors 1 and 3)	29.1	8.5	9.8	33%
Manufactured Products (Sectors 2, 4, 5 and 7)	13.7	7.2	10.1	74%
Total	42.8	15.7	19.9	46%

First of all, the proportion of overall foodstuffs consumption accounted for by imports is enormous: 33% in value terms, a percentage which has no parallel in any other major region of the Third World, where the average (even excluding China) is lower than 10%. A substantial proportion of these inputs, in value terms, is no doubt accounted for by luxury products, but most of them are vital and necessary as a direct result of the inadequacy of local agricultural production.

Secondly, even if one does not include the governments' own consumption of imports, non-foodstuffs imports of consumer goods represent about 50% of household consumption of these products. Here, too, the comparison with other regions of the Third World is striking. The equivalent ratio for Latin America amounts to only 33%, and the figure is considerably lower for Brazil, Mexico and Argentina. In other words, import substitution industrialization is less advanced in the Arab world than in Latin America. The main reason is the relatively small size of each Arab state and perhaps also the higher proportion of luxury goods in the import bill, in relation to the structure of income distribution and the high level of upper income bracket consumption in the Gulf countries.

However, the ratio is actually higher in the rest of the Third World (60% in Black Africa and South, South East and East Asia), where import substitution industrialization is even less advanced. Furthermore, the share of manufactured products as a whole, in total household consumption, is lower in Africa and Asia than in the Arab world (20% as against 32%). This is probably primarily due to the lower level of urbanization in non-Arab Africa and Asia. Also, the general level of consumption is lower and the structure of income distribution less regressive. Imports of manufactured products for consumption are thus a relatively less heavy burden for the national economy in those areas than in the Arab world, in terms of the ratio of these imports to the G.D.P. and the respective countries' import capacity.

In conclusion, one can say that the model of European consumption has made more of a mark upon Arab society than on the other African and Asian countries. This fact, along with the low levels of Arab agricultural production, integrates the region into the world system to a greater extent than other regions of the Third World.

Imports also play a decisive role in the organization of the Arab productive system. Indeed, they provide 55% of requirements for raw materials, semi-finished goods and capital goods — as is clear from the table below.

Arab World's Dependence on Imports for Production Purposes

Category of Good	*Value ($ billions)*		
(a) Consumption of Intermediate Goods	62.5		
(b) Gross Fixed Capital Formation (Sector 7 products)	17.0		
Total	*79.5*		
Imports, c.i.f.			
Intermediate Goods (Sectors 1 to 7)	21.3		
Capital Goods (Sector 7)	14.2		
Imports, in terms of market prices			
Intermediate Goods (Sectors 1 to 7)	26.8	=	43% of (a)
Capital Goods (Sector 7)	17.0	=	100% of (b)
Total	*43.8*	=	*55% of (a+b)*

This extreme dependency is due to the weakness of the Arab mode of industrialization. Light industry remains preponderant (more than 60% of industrial production). The recently established basic industries are more often geared to export than to the satisfaction of the internal needs of production. This is true, for instance, of fertilizer manufacture, of the production of petrochemical materials (plastics) and of the aluminium industry. The development projects of the last decade have accentuated this extraverted orientation of industrialization, which is based entirely on natural resources, mainly energy. This is particularly true in the Gulf.

Under such conditions, no one should be surprised at the

conclusion which stems from the comparison with other regions of the Third World. Firstly, the proportion of imported capital goods, which reaches almost 100% in the Arab world, is of the order of 90% in Asia (India is the only real exception), 100% in non-Arab Africa and 80% in Latin America (where, as in India, there has been some move towards local production of capital goods). Secondly, the proportion of imported inputs (intermediate goods), which reaches 43% in the Arab world, does rise to 66% for Africa (where the level of industrialization is low) but falls to 35% for Asia and 25% for Latin America. Industry is thus less extraverted and less integrated in Asia and Latin America than in the Arab world.

Despite this situation, the overall Arab trade surplus (exports $96.9 billion, imports $51.2 billion) is exceptionally large, representing some 28% of Arab G.D.P. True, this only covers trade in commodities (Sectors 1 to 7) and does not include services. None the less, this surplus, which makes the Arab region a keystone in the equilibrium of the international monetary system, since the bulk of its surplus is recycled and thus compensates for the deficits of other regions of the Third World, bears witness to a level of integration into the world system incomparably greater than any other region of the Third World.

4. Income Distribution and the Structure of Consumption

Returning to Tables 7 and 8, we can take a further step by analysing the structure of consumption in terms of income distribution.

Existing studies of household consumption in the main Arab countries enable us to get some idea of income distribution. The Gini curve, which can be drawn up on the basis of these studies show strong similarities. They all pass close to the same R point (Figure 8 — graph): the consumption of the poorer half of the population being less than a quarter of total consumption.

This is no coincidence, given that, in all the non-desert Arab countries, the rural population represents about half the total population; the few exceptions (the desert countries; Lebanon and Jordan, which are more urbanized than the average; and Mauritania, Yemen and Sudan, which are more rural) carry little demographic weight. In nearly every case the average per capita consumption in the rural areas is about one-third of per capita consumption in the towns. True, rural society is unlikely to be egalitarian. But the richest landowners are probably absentees and the poor (landless labourers, people with tiny plots, and tenants paying in kind) predominate amongst the peasantry. The urban population is even less likely to be homogeneous than the rural population. But the fact remains that most privileged individuals, including the middle strata, are urban.

It is also interesting to note that, while the lower halves of the Gini curves are very similar (from point 0 to point R), the upper halves, from point R upwards, show two distinct modalities. The curve climbs faster in the countries where state intervention and industrialization are relatively advanced than in the countries with a more *laissez-faire* and less industrialized structure. This comes down to saying that reforms and development have reduced inequalities within the upper strata but have done little to change the overall ratio between these strata and the really poor.

We have split household consumption into two components (Columns 2 and 3 of Table 7): consumption which is accounted for in the reconstitution of the value of labour power, and surplus consumption. To do so, we started from the assumption that the per capita consumption corresponding to the poorer half of society represented the minimum consumption necessary to reproduce labour power. This consumption — $170 per head, or $645 per economically active individual — was allocated amongst the various sector categories in proportion to the corresponding data for the approximately equivalent income stratum in the consumption studies. The difference between each pair of entries is equivalent to surplus consumption. The sum of necessary consumption plus surplus consumption gives us total household consumption, which emerges as an average of $370 per capita or $1,400 per economically active individual.

Although very rough, this method serves as an essential tool for any eventual development policy genuinely geared to satisfying the needs of the masses rather than simply to maximizing overall consumption, including surplus consumption, which is equivalent to a maximization of growth within the existing structures. It will also enable us to analyse the use the Arab system makes of labour power to satisfy the different needs of society.

5. The Use of Arab Labour Power

In Tables 12, 13 and 14, we have laid out the way jobs requiring different levels of skill are distributed across the 11 sectors under consideration. The statistics for non-agricultural labour are set out in Table 12. Table 13 correlates employment figures (aggregated for agriculture, and for public and domestic services, and broken down for industrial sectors 3 to 7) with the value added by each of the various sectors. It emerges that value added per economically active individual is of the order of $400 in agriculture and $4,000 in non-agricultural activities, excluding oil.

Table 14 breaks down the distribution of employment into three levels of qualification corresponding to educational experience: illiterate or primary school only, secondary school, and technical or university level. The respective overall percentages for these categories are 87%, 8.3% and 4.8%.

We then set out to calculate the direct and indirect labour content required from each level of qualification in order to satisfy society's needs. To do so, we defined three types of social needs, represented by the Vertical Vectors D1, D2 and D3 in Table 15 — D1 = consumption necessary for the reproduction of labour power ($24.4 billion); D2 = surplus consumption ($24.5 billion); D3 = indirect requirements, made up of (i) administrative consumption, (ii) gross fixed capital formation, (iii) exports in excess of imports (in all, $106.3 billion).

The square section of Table 15 is based on the matrix of technical coefficients in the 11 sector table, the vertical vectors of Final Demand D1, D2 and D3 and their sum, D. The Horizontal Vectors, E, E1, E2 and E3, represent the number of jobs (in thousands) per $billion of production for each sector. Vector E corresponds to total employment and Vectors E1, E2 and E3 correspond to the various levels of education, as outlined above.

Table 16 is an industrial table, aggregated for greater simplicity into five sectors derived from those in Table 11. Table 17 presents the elements for a calculation of labour incorporated in the five sectors, and corresponds to Table 15, which provides the same elements for eleven sectors.

On the basis of Table 17, we can calculate the $1\text{-}A^{-1}$ matrix:

$$1\text{-}A^{-1} = 1 + A + A^2 + A^3 + \ldots$$

which gives us:

1.177	0.006	0.237	0.071	0.019
0.023	1.109	0.050	0.049	0.065
0.122	0.052	1.532	0.648	0.180
0.002	0.001	0.005	1.001	0.021
0.193	0.056	0.521	0.271	1.203

The three matrices for incorporated labour, T1, T2 and T3, can then be calculated as $T = E\ 1\text{-}A^{-1}$, with E being each of the three diagonal matrices for employment per $billion of production, E1, E2 and E3. Thus:

(a) $T1 = E1\ 1\text{-}A^{-1}$

	1,883,200	9,600	379,200	113,600	30,400
	0.073	3,527	0,159	0,156	0,207
	5,368	2,288	67,408	28,152	7,920
	0,136	0,068	0,340	68,068	1,428
	9,225	2,677	24,904	12,954	57,503
Total	*1,898,002*	*18,158*	*472,010*	*223,288*	*97,458*

(b) $T2 = E2\ 1\text{-}A^{-1}$

	0	0	0	0	0
	0,022	1,064	0,048	0,047	0,062
	1,696	0,723	21,295	9,007	2,502
	0,012	0,007	0,031	6,206	0,130
	11,387	3,304	30,739	15,989	70,977
Total	*13,117*	*5,097*	*52,112*	*31,249*	*73,671*

(c) T3 = E3 1-A^{-1}

	0	0	0	0	0
	0,009	0,450	0,021	0,020	0,027
	0,682	0,292	8,570	3,628	0,900
	0,008	0,004	0,020	4,004	0,082
	6,770	1,970	18,400	9,500	42,300
Total	*7,469*	*2,716*	*27,011*	*17,152*	*43,309*

T1, T2 and T3, the direct and indirect labour incorporated in Demands D1, D2 and D3, are obtained by multiplying the elements in the columns in each T matrix by the elements which respectively make up the Final Demands D1, D2 and D3. Thus:

(a) Low Level Qualifications:

	T1D1	*T1D2*	*T1D3*
	12,147	7,028	5,964
	9	29	1,503
	7,410	6,797	–5,475
	66	156	4,488
	146	350	458
Total	*19,778*	*14,360*	*6,668*

(b) Middle Level Qualifications:

	T2D1	*T2D2*	*T2D3*
	84	55	4
	3	8	422
	818	750	–604
	9	22	628
	110	265	346
Total	*1,025*	*1,101*	*796*

(c) Higher Level Qualifications:

	T3D1	T3D2	T3D3
	47	32	2
	1	4	224
	424	388	–313
	5	12	344
	64	155	203
Total	*543*	*592*	*462*

We can then proceed to the following double entry table (thousands of jobs):

	Labour Incorporated in Demand			
Level of Qualification of Labour Involved	*D1*	*D2*	*D3*	*D (Total)*
T1	20,400	15,800	6,930	43,130
T2	1,175	1,275	919	3,369
T3	630	688	533	1,851
Total T	*22,205*	*17,763*	*8,382*	*48,350*

Column D corresponds to the manning levels for each level of qualification in Table 16. The reader will note that the figures differ slightly from those obtained by the calculation above, a divergence due to the approximate character of the calculation of the matrix $1\text{-}A^{-1}$.

We can now introduce employment: firstly, in the public sector (a component of D3); and secondly, domestic employment (a component of D2), which gives us:

Labour Incorporated in Final Demand (Thousands of Jobs)

	D1		*D2*		*D3*		*D*	
	Jobs	*%*	*Jobs*	*%*	*Jobs*	*%*	*Jobs*	*%*
T1	20,400	91.7	18,450	90.3	7,570	70.1	46,420	86.9
T2	1,175	5.4	1,275	6.3	1,969	18.4	4,429	8.3
T3	630	2.9	688	3.4	1,233	11.5	2,551	4.8
Total	*22,205*	*100*	*20,413*	*100*	*10,782*	*100*	*53,400*	*100*

Distribution of Labour Elements Incorporated, Relative to Total Labour Force (53,400 Thousand Jobs)

	D1	*D2*	*D3*	*D*
T1	38.0	34.0	14.7	86.7
T2	2.2	2.4	3.8	8.4
T3	1.2	1.3	2.4	4.9
T (Total)	*41.4*	*37.7*	*20.9*	*100*

Distribution of Labour Elements Incorporated According to Level of Qualification

	D1	*D2*	*D3*	*D*
T1	43.5	39.9	16.6	100
T2	26.5	29.8	43.7	100
T3	24.8	26.9	48.3	100
T (Total)	*41.4*	*37.7*	*20.9*	*100*

These results enable us to assess the kind of distortion in the employment of labour which flows from the modalities of the Arab economy's integration into the world system.

D3		*D*	
Jobs	*%*	*Jobs*	*%*
7,570	70.1	46,420	86.9
1,979	18.4	4,429	8.3
1,223	11.5	2,551	4.8
10,782	*100*	*53,400*	*100*

As far as the use of the labour force as a whole is concerned, the comparison between the Arab system and that in force in the developed countries is particularly instructive. The table below is for France in 1971 and is fairly indicative of the situation in the developed world. The figures are from Baudelot, Establet and Toisier, *Qui travaille pour qui?* (Paris, 1979), p. 180.

	Arab Economy 1976	*France 1971*
Use of the Labour force for the satisfaction of:		
D1 (consumption)	41.4%	49.8%
D2 (surplus consumption)	37.7%	9.6%
D3 (indirect demand)	20.9%	40.6%
Total Labour	*100*	*100*

It emerges that the productive apparatus of the developed countries is mainly oriented towards the requirements of reproducing labour power and only secondarily towards surplus consumption. On the other hand, state intervention and the level of accumulation are higher for these countries than in the Arab world (41% as against 21%), but they ensure the reproduction of a D1/D2 ratio more favourable to D1 (D1/D1 + D2 = 84% as against 52% in the Arab world). In contrast, the Arab system appears to be geared more to the satisfaction of surplus consumption.

The smaller proportion of labour directed to indirect demand in the Arab world also calls for some comment.

The labour allocated to the state (state employees and agents, plus labour involved in the state's current consumption of goods and services) is similarly geared to permit the reproduction of the social system and development within that system.

But what about the labour force allocated to export-oriented production? Where exports and imports are roughly equal in value, it might be considered that the labour deployed to produce exports is used to pay for the imports. One might then compare the amount of labour incorporated in our exports with that incorporated in the foreign production which provides our imports, and thus measure the degree of equality (or inequality) in the value of the exchange. If exports are higher (or lower) in value than imports, we might reduce (or increase) them proportionately to establish the comparison. But it is worth bearing in mind that a trade surplus can, as in the Arab case, constitute a placement abroad, which is in turn one element in the reproduction of the system.

In the Arab world, oil exports incorporate only a very small quantity of labour (direct and indirect). Yet these exports pay for imports (and a surplus to boot) which incorporate a much greater quantity of labour. This is precisely the 'comparative advantage' invoked by those who justify participation in the international division of labour. The comparison of the quantities of labour exchanged may even be interpreted as 'unequal exchange' in favour of the Arab world. Such a conclusion would, of course, be over hasty, since we are talking of a non-renewable resource, and oil revenues are supposed to compensate for its exhaustion. None the less, precisely because Vector D3 is so constituted (the algebraic sum of public sector consumption plus accumulation plus exports, less imports), the proportion of labour incorporated to satisfy Demand D3 is lower in the Arab world than in the developed West.

If we reduce D3 to only two elements, state activities and accumulation, leaving out foreign trade, the distribution of incorporated labour would look like this:

Sector	*D3 (restricted)*	*T1D3*	*T2D3*	*T3D3*	*TD3*
1	0	0	0	0	0
2	1.5	27	7	4	38
3	24.5	11,600	1,250	660	13,510
4	20.2	4,460	630	340	5,420
5	4.4	428	320	190	938
Total	*50.6*	*16,515*	*2,197*	*1,194*	*19,906*

The structure of the distribution of labour would then appear more similar, in so far as Vector D3 is concerned, to that of the developed world. But the distortion in the D1/D2 ratio would remain.

Distribution of Incorporated Labour

	D3 (Complete) Total Quantity of Labour	%	*D3 (Restricted)* Total Quantity of Labour	%	Developed Countries %
D1	22,205	41.4	22,205	34.0	49.8
D2	20,413	37.7	20,413	31.4	9.6
D3	10,782	20.9	22,306	40.6	40.6
D	*53,400*	*100*	*64,924*	*100*	*100*

Foreign trade obviously enables the Arab world to 'economize' the difference, amounting to 11,524 thousand workers per year. However, this figure is not particularly meaningful. The labour incorporated in the imports considered in the calculation for D3 (complete) is not the foreign labour in fact incorporated in these imports but the local (Arab) labour which would have to be allocated to satisfy the demand if the imports were eliminated and replaced with local products. Thus, the assumption is that each sector could produce a complete range of import substitutes. Such an assumption may be warranted when one compares two developed economies, each of which produces more or less everything they need apart from a few raw materials (for instance, Europe and the U.S.). But this is not the case when one is comparing the Arab world with 'the rest of the world'. One can then only say that oil exports make possible the importation of many goods, whether analogous or not to those produced in the Arab world, which cost or would cost a considerable amount of labour. Less obviously, one can also say that the 'labour economies' which the Arab world's participation in the international division of labour permit (whatever their volume) are allocated to satisfy surplus consumption, D2, and not to necessary consumption, D1.

Furthermore, the Arab system, as opposed to that which prevails in the developed West, exhibits a specific and systematic distortion in the proportion of qualified labour used to meet indirect demand and the requirements of surplus consumption.

In the Arab economy, Demand D1 (reproduction of labour power) absorbs 41.4% of total labour, including 26.5% of middle-level qualified labour and 24.8% of highly qualified labour. Demand D2 (surplus consumption) absorbs 37.7% of total labour, including 29.8% of middle-level qualified labour and 26.9% of highly qualified labour. Demand D3 (indirect) absorbs 20.9% of total labour, including 43.7% of middle-level qualified labour and 48.3% of highly qualified labour.

Qualified labour is much less unequally distributed amongst the different types of demand in a country like France, for instance. Thus, in the French example quoted earlier, we find 49.8% of the labour force allocated to consumption and 9.6% to surplus consumption. Of these, middle-level cadres account for 9.9% of incorporated labour, representing 4.9% of the labour force. Higher level cadres account for 5.3% of incorporated labour, representing 2.7% of the labour force. In France, the reproduction of labour power, which absorbs 49.8% of the overall labour force, accounts for 45% of middle ranking cadres' labour and 46% of higher cadres' labour.

Qualified labour is considered to be a scarce resource, the lack of which leads to bottlenecks which slow down growth. Yet this scarce resource is particularly ill-employed in the Arab world, where little of it is allocated to meet the needs of the masses and a great deal to fulfil the direct or indirect requirements of the privileged.

A brief comment seems called for at this point. What sense is there, one may ask, in calculating an 'Arab average' based on an overall inter-industrial table which brings together data from 20 countries as different from one another as the Arab countries are? The answer is that the distortion we have noted is not only common to all the relevant countries under consideration, it is also an indicator of the course their evolution is taking. Had we made the same calculations for each country individually, we would have discovered that the distortion was greater in Egypt than in the Sudan, in Iraq than in Egypt, and in Kuwait than in Iraq. In other words, the higher one goes up the development ladder, as measured by G.D.P., the more marked is the distortion. The average, which is in any case higher than for the other regions of the Third World, is a clear indicator of the direction development is taking. In this sense, it is highly significant.

6. Conclusion: Integration into the World System and Multinational Domination over the Arab Economy

Questions concerning the relations which express the multinationals' domination over the contemporary economies of Third World states are often approached from a micro-economic viewpoint, in the sense that what is examined is the domination exercised by one particular multinational, or group thereof, over a specific sector or country. For instance, such studies concentrate on the workings of the aluminium industry or the banana market, and bring out the decisive role played by the monopolies that dominate this industry or that market. Studies of this kind are valuable and have contributed greatly to our understanding of the realities of the contemporary world economic system. However, they are not enough if we are to grasp the overall workings of the mechanisms of accumulation and development on a world scale. To appreciate fully how these mechanisms operate, we must not only take a *macro*-economic view, we must also take into account the relevant social and political factors.

Sector by sector analyses of the domination exercised by the multinationals over the various sectors and industries are already more fruitful than the traditional analyses that are confined to an inventory of property. However, especially in the Arab world, political consciousness has not developed any further than this: foreign domination is thus accounted for solely in terms of foreign appropriation. Of course, foreign ownership of capital was the dominant factor for a considerable period, from the late 19th Century to the 1950s and 1960s. In French North Africa, this appropriation extended not only to all industrial activity but also to the major part of commercial agricultural production (the 'lands of settlement'), and even to petty commodity production in all the other sectors dominated by the settlers' small- and medium-scale enterprises. In Egypt, foreign capital, associated with monopolistic Egyptian private capital (the Misr Group) dominated every sector of industry, banking, trade and modern services; foreign settlements were for a long time predominant in capitalist petty production as well. Only agriculture, which was still organized in latifundia, escaped direct foreign appropriation. In the Ottoman Empire, and then in the states that succeeded it, foreign appropriation was more limited and developed later, but it none the less gradually spread from the service sector to industry. Finally, oil production was directly dominated by a cartel of American, British and French companies. Any analysis of the Arab economy around 1950 would reveal the massive and decisive scale of this foreign appropriation.

Formal Foreign Ownership No Longer the Central Issue
However, all this is no longer the case today. Formal foreign ownership almost disappeared during specific periods in certain countries (in Egypt, for instance, from 1957 to 1971). The exodus of the foreign settlers (notably from North Africa), the systematic nationalization of foreign businesses and even of substantial sectors of national capital — first in Egypt, then in Syria, Iraq, Algeria, Libya, Tunisia, Sudan and Democratic Yemen — have transformed the structures of ownership. But the tendency for state capitalism to replace the old mix of foreign and private local capital as the dominant form of ownership is not prevalent only in those Arab countries that have opted for a socialist course. It operates with equal force in the other countries, from Morocco to the Gulf states. The nationalization of sub-soil assets and oil production has progressed steadily in the same direction throughout the 1960s and 1970s.

Gradually, once formal ownership had been recovered, it emerged that, because of the participation of the Arab economies in the world system, the capital of the monopolies that dominated this system on a world scale continued to dominate the Arab economies. This awareness is, however, quite recent and remains restricted mainly to professional circles.

New Forms of Domination by Multinationals

Various aspects of this new form of domination are beginning to be known. Firstly, there is technological dependency. The latter, which is far from being simply moral and intellectual, is manifest in: (1) the very high monopoly prices imposed by the multinationals for industrial plant and strategic inputs to the production process (engineering, industrial know-how, agribusiness inputs, etc.); (2) the multinationals' refusal to sell technological equipment piecemeal and their insistence that complete and complex installations be purchased on a turnkey basis; (3) their refusal to sell those technological inputs which enable them to maintain control over the productive process as a whole. The Arab states are still compelled to import practically all their industrial means of production. Furthermore, the kind of agricultural development that is being envisaged will involve increasing recourse to multinational agribusiness.

Every Arab enterprise, whether privately or publicly owned, is thus forced to remain dependent on the multinationals. The massive purchase of turnkey factories, as practised by the richer countries who thereby hope to accelerate their own development, has repeatedly been the subject of critical analyses. Of course, it is difficult to estimate just how much value is transferred in the course of these transactions, as the transfer of profits is not often incorporated into the original asking price, unlike in previous times when, under the old forms of foreign ownership, at least part of the transfer of profits could be ascertained from the companies' accounts. But the quantities involved are clearly considerable. Recourse to foreign loans and to suppliers' credits — usually private — in order to facilitate the purchase of the means of production constitutes *the* major factor in the acceleration of the Third World's foreign debt.

Orientation of production towards export industries further accentuates this costly dependency. The Arab countries have opted for this course, to the great detriment of autocentric development, as a way of going beyond the import substitution stage. The financially well-off Arab states have chosen to base these export industries on the exploitation of their natural resources (for example, plastics, fertilizers and aluminium in the Gulf countries). The rest have sought to build up industries based on cheap labour (for example, the Suez Canal free trade zone in Egypt, textiles and clothing in Morocco and Tunisia). The extreme technological dependence imposed by the intended destination of the product in both the above cases is thus supplemented by the multinationals' control over marketing.

We can now situate the dependency of the Arab economy on dominant monopoly capital in terms of its proper historical context. From this standpoint, the formation of the contemporary world system has gone through three stages, corresponding to three different modalities of integration of the dominated periphery.

The Three Phases of Integrating the Dominated Periphery

The first phase, characterized by the gradual expansion on a world scale of the commodity market covered the whole of the 19th Century and beyond. A specific international division of labour was established within this framework, but production for export in the periphery was still organized within the framework of autonomous modes of production. In some cases, the dominant classes themselves opted for integration into the new system and modified the way production was organized accordingly. The classical examples are the transformation of land tenure and the development of cotton production in Egypt from 1860 to the turn of the century, and to a lesser extent the organization of export-oriented agricultural production in the Ottoman Levant. Iraq underwent a similar transformation between the wars. In French North Africa and in Palestine, this production for export was organized directly by settlers, on lands expropriated from the peoples of the region.

The second phase was characterized by the gradual expansion on a world scale of the capital market. The centralization of capital had, by the end of the 19th Century, reached a sufficiently high level for capital to be exported and foreign units of capitalist production to be implanted. This classical phase of imperialism lasted up until the 1950s and 1960s in the Arab world. The foreign units of capitalist production, which began by taking over the commercial and financial sectors associated with export specialization, gradually extended their hold to cover import substitution industries, notably in Egypt and the Arab East during the Second World War. But these units maintained a certain autonomy *vis-a-vis* the metropolitan monopolies, even when they were subsidiaries of financial consortia. Nationalist critiques of foreign domination developed during this phase and the theme of nationalization eventually came to the fore, without engendering a clear awareness of the limits inherent in this substitution of national state ownership for ownership by foreign capital.

The third phase in this evolution has barely begun. It constitutes a more advanced stage in the international division of labour, characterized by the break-up of the world productive system into separate units which are geographically dispersed amongst the countries of the centre and the periphery, yet none the less follow a single overall strategy.

This break-up of the world productive system is based on the dominant capital's maximum exploitation of 'comparative advantage'. The latter depends partly on the exploitation of the different conditions prevailing in the labour market and partly on the appropriation of revenues connected with the availability of natural resources. It amounts to the extension on a world scale of the labour market, and thereby completes the trilogy: commodities, capital, labour. The overall domination of capital can operate through formal appropriation of the various sections of the productive apparatus by the multinationals; but it can operate just as effectively even if formal ownership of certain sections is relinquished, providing control over strategic elements in the process, notably, the production of the most modern means of production, is retained. We have already described the symptoms of the particularly extensive integration of the Arab economy into the contemporary world system. The weakness of the Arab economy is a direct consequence.

The Consequent Weaknesses of the Arab Economy at the Present Time

The first weakness is the total disarticulation of the various industrial systems, which is manifest in the weakness of inter-industrial exchange of locally produced inputs and plant. Corresponding to this disarticulation, we find that the Arab political world is usually inclined to reject arguments as to the necessity of technological autonomy. The latter is generally considered to be either quite impossible or a mere expression of cultural nationalism, rather than a social and economic necessity. Development plans articulated around industrialization for export further accentuate this disarticulation.

The second weakness is the persistent backwardness of agriculture, which remains the poor relation in development policies, while industry absorbs all the financial and other resources. Apart from the social obstacles which stand in the way of any modernization of agriculture, the exploitation of the rural areas to the greater benefit of dependent industrial accumulation aggravates the nutritional deficit and reduces the potentialities of the local market. Once again, development projects revolving round large-scale programmes and the use of imported technology will inevitably accentuate the domination of the agribusiness multinationals without providing any decisive solution to the fundamental problems.

The third weakness is the increasingly unequal distribution of income domestically, as integration into the international division of labour proceeds. This regressive distribution is accompanied by massive adoption of European modes of consumption. It shrinks the market for goods which are essential to the satisfaction of needs and orients development towards increasingly disarticulated types of production grafted on to the world system.

The fourth weakness is that the growing distortion in the overall orientation of development is accompanied by a parallel regressive distortion in the allocation of scarce resources, especially skilled labour.

The fifth weakness is that, given these conditions, the Arab system is incapable of using the resources so amply available to it, notably the financial resources provided by the export of oil and natural gas, to further its own development. This incapacity, aggravated as it is by the political fragmentation of the Arab world (which is maintained by extraverted development), integrates the region still further into the world system by imposing specific functions upon it within the international monetary equilibrium.

These are the objective bases of multinational monopoly capital's domination over the Arab economy as a whole, not just over this or that sector or business considered in isolation. The same applies to another area of the Third World, the four East Asian countries (South Korea, Taiwan, Hong Kong and Singapore) whose development is also based on maximally disarticulated industrialization. (The best study illustrating the fragility of the South Korean 'economic miracle' as compared to the prodigious autocentric development of North Korea is *Korea, North and South*, by Gavan McCormack, Mark Selden et al., New York, Monthly Review Press, 1978.)

In Latin America, on the other hand, the local industrial systems, which, incidentally, are more advanced than those of the Arab world, although still dominated by the monopolies at the technological level, are on the whole less disarticulated and indeed more integrated, especially in Brazil. In Black Africa, South and South East Asia, industry is generally more embryonic (except in India, in absolute terms), agriculture is more backward, and the distribution of income is regressive. However, in each of these regions, the process of regressive development is, in the last analysis, less advanced than in the Arab world.

Arab history does not, of course, begin with oil, nor does the history of its integration as a periphery dominated by imperialism. None the less, oil has certainly accentuated the distortions of dependent Arab development, both before, and especially after, 1973.

While creating the illusion of wealth, oil has rather the same effect on the Arab world, as South American gold had on Spain in the 17th Century: it delays the fundamental changes that are necessary for any genuine Arab renaissance.

It is not true that the Arab countries are preparing for the years when the oil has run out. The oil-rich countries (our Group A) are increasingly neglecting the activities which have provided their livelihood until recently. When they do attend to such problems, it is only to set up development projects based precisely on the continuation of the present system. For example, how many irrigation programmes are based on cheap energy, in other words, on oil? As the black gold runs out, the newly cultivated areas will thus inevitably return to the desert. As for the semi-oil producing countries (Group B), these are not envisaging anything which has not already been tried in Egypt. Should their oil income start to fall, they would face similar disaster. Finally, the non-oil producing states (Groups C and D) are simply trying to survive, staving off disaster with what little of the oil revenues finds its way into their countries. The similarity of all these situations does not create unity or solidarity. The whole superficial edifice built on a non-renewable resource is totally unstable.

Oil revenues invested abroad are not a source of future security either. It seems quite possible that, once the oil has dried up and the Arab world no longer disposes of its most useful means of pressure upon the West, the Western countries will find a way of 'nationalizing' these financial investments. The comparison with other OPEC countries is instructive. The table below shows the make-up of the G.D.P. of various countries in 1975—78.

Sectoral Composition of G.D.P. (%)

	Venezuela	*Nigeria*	*Indonesia*	*Iran*
(1) Agriculture	6	26	31	9
(2) Mines, oil	23	30	19	40
(3) Industry	17	7	9	10
(4) Exports	32	35	22	40
(5) Imports	27	32	21	32
(6) Gross Fixed Capital Formation	31	31	21	25

Of course, these countries exhibit certain similarities with the Arab world: the decisive role of oil production, and hence of exports; the commercial surplus; the high level of investment. None the less, Venezuela is relatively more industrialized, while Indonesia and Nigeria have a higher agricultural output. As one looks closer, one sees that the analogy based simply on the role of oil is very limited.

On the other hand, the analogy between the present situation of the Arab world and that of Iran [before the Revolution *Publisher's Note*] is striking. Iran's turnover, equivalent in scale to about one-quarter of the Arab world's, has a remarkably similar structure: industrial disarticulation, extreme backwardness of agriculture, maximally regressive distribution of income, incredible distortions in the allocation of resources, etc. The lesson is worth drawing.

The internal development policies implemented in the Arab world over the last 30 years, both before and after 1973, have always been presented as a means of accelerating growth and catching up with the overall structures of the developed world (in terms of technology, industrialization, urbanization, pattern of consumption and standard of living), and as a way of moving gradually from dependency to independence. However, if one examines the facts, it emerges that the acceleration of growth has not proceeded as expected. On the contrary, the qualitative gap has widened in every domain and the weaknesses of the Arab world have grown. Dependency has changed form and has got worse in the process. The apparent wealth provided by oil from 1973 onwards, has of course, accelerated growth, but in a regressive direction; it is indubitably the root cause of the Arab world's increasingly unequal integration into the world system.

The Only Alternative

The alternative is obviously a development that is autocentric and oriented to the needs of the masses. This would imply: (1) a drastic re-orientation of priorities in favour of agriculture and the kind of industrialization which helps to develop agriculture and satisfy the needs of the broad masses of the population; (2) a fundamental revision of the technological options; (3) a change in the allocation of scarce resources, notably skilled labour, and probably a re-examination of the form and content of professional qualifications; (4) a selective disconnection and corresponding reduction of the Arab productive system's integration into a world system dominated by multinational monopolies. We have dealt extensively with these problems in *La Crise de L'Imperialisme* and *Imperialism and Unequal Development*.

It is easy to say that the alternative we propose here is unrealistic, impossible, utopian. It is true that it does not correspond to the programme of any significant political force at the present time, or even of any likely force whatsoever. But it does correspond to the objective interests of the Arab peoples, and thereby qualifies as a possible and indeed objectively necessary alternative form of development.

Because the existing political forces operating within the Arab world will not envisage this other option, the Arab peoples' rejection of the model proposed to them in various forms by their rulers may well engender a populist revolt. The example of Iran is there to prove it, and clearly expresses what it is that the people have rejected, for all that they are, for the time being, incapable of formulating a coherent strategy of their own. However, despite the ideological ambiguities, the political blind alleys, the steps forward followed by sudden retreats, there is every reason to believe that the forces moving towards a different kind of development may crystallize in the turbulent course of populist revolt. It would not be the first time that history had moved forward in this way.

Statistical Appendix

Table 1
Gross Domestic Product, and Total and Economically Active Population

	G.D.P. (1976) ($000 million)	Total Population (1976) (000)	Economically Active Population (1977) Total (000)	Economically Active Population (1977) In Agriculture (%)
1. Algeria	16,497	17,300	3,744	53
2. Morocco	8,083	17,830	4,872	52.9
3. Tunisia	4,450	5,740	1,446	43.2
4. Mauritania	435	1,350	461	84.3
5. Libya	14,164	2,510	650	19.7
6. Egypt	14,905	37,870	10,427	51.6
7. Sudan	5,064	16,130	5,065	78.5
8. Jordan	1,206	2,780	691	28.1
9. Syria	5,904	7,600	1,998	48.6
10. Lebanon	14,667	2,961	793	12.4
11. Iraq	15,690	11,510	2,955	42.1
12. Saudi Arabia	43,924	9,240	2,001	62.0
13. Kuwait	12,144	1,031	312	1.7
14. Bahrain	1,195	259	60	6.6
15. Qatar	2,864	95	90	(7)
16. United Arab Emirates	9,710	229	(56)	(7)
17. Oman	2,318	791	214	63.4
18. Yemen	1,857	6,870	1,578	76.3
19. Democratic Yemen	292	1,750	462	60.5
Total	*162,169*	*143,846*	*37,875*	*56*

Source: Trade and Development Statistics Manual (UNCTAD, 1979)

Table 2
Sectorial Composition of G.D.P. (%)

	(1) *Agriculture, Forestry, Fisheries*	(2) *Mining, Electricity, Oil*	(3) *Manufacturing*	(4) *Construction*	(5) *Trade*	(6) *Transport and Communications*	(7) *Other*
1. Algeria (1976)	8	26	13	13	11	7	15
2. Morocco (1975)	24	9	15	9	24	-------- 19 --------	
3. Tunisia (1976)	17	8	9	9		5	34[1]
4. Mauritania (1973)	23	33	5	5	8	6	15
5. Libya (1975)	3	51	2	11	6	7	17
6. Egypt (1975)	30	5	17	4	14	5	23
7. Sudan (1974)	79	2	9	4	16	6	18
8. Jordan (1975)	15	5	12	5	16	8	27
9. Syria (1976)	22	11	11	7	20	5	24
10. Lebanon (1972)	10		16[2]	5	32	8	31
11. Iraq (1975)	7	57	6	2	5	4	17
12. Saudi Arabia (1976)	1	71	5	7	3	4	9
13. Kuwait (1975)	0	72	5	1	6	3	13
17. Oman (1975)	2	65	0	12	7	3	11
18. Yemen (1973)	61	1	2	4	15	2	1
19. Democratic Yemen (1970)	19	2	25	1	13	5	35

Sources: *U.N. Yearbook of National Accounts*, Vol. II (1976), Table 3 (G.D.P.).
Notes: 1. Including Sector 5.
2. Including Sector 2.
Total not always equal to 100 as import duties not always included.

Table 3
Uses of G.D.P. (%)

	(1) Administration	(2) Private Consumption	(3) Gross Fixed Capital Formation	(4) Exports	(5) Imports
1. Algeria (1976)	14	46	46	33	40
2. Morocco (1975)	16	71	26	27	41
3. Tunisia (1976)	15	62	30	29	37
4. Mauritania (1973)	16	52	33	49	51
5. Libya (1975)	27	37	28	53	46
6. Egypt (1975)	25	68	25	19	40
7. Sudan (1974)	14	77	14	12	21
8. Jordan (1975)	38	92	29	42	99
9. Syria (1976)	20	60	35	23	39
10. Lebanon (1972)	9	87	20	58	45
11. Iraq (1975)	9	51[2]	27	--------- 16 ---------[1]	
12. Saudi Arabia (1976)	18	12	22	78	31
13. Kuwait (1975)	16	18	8	81	22
17. Oman (1975)	44	11	30	66	51
18. Yemen (1973)	10	97	10	3	22

Sources: see Table 2.
Notes: 1. Exports less imports.
2. Including administration.

Table 4
The Arab World as a Whole, 1976 ($000 Millions)

	(1) ($000 millions)	(2) %	(3) Manufacturing %	(4) Industries ($000 millions)
Sources of G.D.P.				
1. Agriculture, forestry, fisheries	14.7	9.1		
2. Mining, oil, electricity, water	82.1	51.1		
3/7. Manufacturing	11.6	7.2		
Agriculture			30.5	3,630
Tobacco			22.4	2,600
Textiles, leather			4.4	510
Wood, woodworking			3.0	350
Paper, printing			17.0	1,880
Chemicals and petrochemicals			7.0	810
Processing of non-metallic minerals			1.4	160
Base metals			13.4	1,560
Engineering			0.9	100
Other Industries				
8. Construction, public works	10.0	6.2		
9. Transport and communications	7.2	4.5		
10. Trade	10.9	6.8		
11. Services (excluding government)	8.7	5.4		
Administration	13.0	8.1		
Domestic services	4.0	2.5		
Total G.D.P.	*162.2*	*100.0*		
Employment				
Private consumption	52.9	32.8		
Public consumption				
Goods and services	14.6	9.1		
Salaries	13.0	8.0		
Gross Fixed Capital Formation	36.0	22.4		
Exports	96.9	60.0		
Less Imports	—51.2	—31.8		

Notes and Sources:
Column (1): calculated from Tables 1, 2 and 3.
Column (3): Source: I.D.C.A.S. in G.P. Casadio, *The Economic Challenge of the Arabs* (Saxon House, 1976), Table 6.2

abs

Industrial sectors retained in tables below:

3. Agriculture, foodstuffs, drinks, tobacco $3.600 million
4. Other light industries: textiles, leather, wood paper — $3.600 million
5. Chemicals and petrochemicals — $1.900 million
6. Non-metallic materials — $0.800 million
7. Metals, engineering — $1.700 million

Table 5
Composition of Imports (%)

	(1) Foodstuffs	*(2)* Raw Materials and Semi-finished Goods	*(3)* Fuels	*(4)* Machinery	*(5)* Transport Equipment	*(6)* Consumer Goods
1. Algeria (1973)	14.2	35.6	1.4	27.0	14.0	7.7
2. Morocco (1975)	28.2	27.6	10.7	17.3	11.5	4.3
3. Tunisia (1976)	12.1	33.3	11.5	23.8	11.0	8.1
4. Mauritania (1972)	22.2	19.5	6.1	27.1	19.2	5.5
5. Libya (1975)	14.8	35.8	1.6	20.2	12.2	15.4
6. Egypt (1976)	22.0	37.5	5.5	17.7	12.6	4.6
7. Sudan (1975)	17.5	37.8	3.4	15.6	18.3	7.0
8. Jordan (1975)	20.5	24.6	10.6	14.1	17.5	11.3
9. Syria (1975)	18.0	37.0	6.4	14.2	14.8	9.5
10. Lebanon (1973)	15.5	39.3	4.7	11.8	12.6	15.9
11. Iraq (1975)	17.1	37.1	0.0	18.6	22.1	5.0
12. Saudi Arabia (1974)	17.1	26.7	0.9	17.5	19.0	18.4
13. Kuwait (1975)	15.3	20.1	0.6	13.8	28.9	22.7
14. Bahrain (1975)	5.6	15.8	50.3	12.3	4.4	11.7
15. Qatar (1975)	13.0	23.2	1.0	19.1	18.3	24.8
18. Yemen (1975)	42.9	21.7	5.0	5.4	9.2	15.7

Source: Yearbook of International Trade, 1976, Vol. I.
Note: When applied to volume of trade for 1976, these proportions give us the following distribution ($000 millions):

Imports (sectors)	*(1)*	*(2)*	*(3)*	*(4)*	*(5)*	*(6)*	*Total*
Sectors:							
1. Agricultural products (unprocessed)	4.0	—	—	—	—	—	*4.0*
2. Mining, oil, electricity	—	4.0	2.5	—	—	—	*6.5*
3. Agricultural and food-processing industry	4.5	—	—	—	—	—	*4.5*
4. Other light industry	—	—	—	—	—	3.2	*3.2*
5. Chemicals	—	5.5	—	—	—	0.5	*6.0*
6. Building Materials	—	2.5	—	—	—	—	*2.5*
7. Metals, engineering	—	4.0	—	9.5	8.5	2.5	*24.5*
Total	*8.5*	*16.0*	*2.5*	*9.5*	*8.5*	*6.2*	*51.2*

Table 6
Composition of Exports (%)

	(1) Agricultural Products	(2) Minerals, Oil	(3) Manufactures	(4) of which: Agricultural and Food-Processing Industries	(5) Textiles	(6) Chemicals
1. Algeria (1973)	2.6	79.3	18.0	9.9	0.6	5.3
2. Morocco (1975)	16.9	58.9	24.2	0.5	7.7	3.6
3. Tunisia (1976)	4.8	50.0	45.2	16.0	12.8	11.9
4. Mauritania (1972)	10.3	81.3	8.4	3.1	0.1	0.0
5. Libya (1975)	0.0	98.5	1.5	0.0	0.0	1.5
6. Egypt (1976)	42.5	18.8	38.7	4.4	19.5	9.5
7. Sudan (1975)	87.1	0.5	12.4	8.1	0.5	3.7
8. Jordan (1975)	24.3	49.8	26.2	5.2	5.0	7.0
9. Syria (1975)	16.8	70.8	12.4	3.0	6.2	1.5
10. Lebanon (1973)	17.2	0.4	82.4	9.1	13.9	9.8
11. Iraq (1975)	38.7	3.7	57.8	9.8	0.8	43.9
12. Saudi Arabia (1974)	0.1	94.3	5.6	0.0	0.0	5.5
13. Kuwait (1975)	0.2	82.7	17.2	0.2	0.4	13.6
14. Bahrain (1975)	0.7	0.9	98.2	0.8	3.4	81.0
17. Oman (1975)	0.2	99.8	0.0	0.0	0.0	0.0
18. Yemen (1975)	70.1	0.0	29.8	17.9	8.9	1.8

Source: Yearbook of International Trade, 1976, Vol. I.
Note: Proportions for groups (1), (3), (4), (5) and (6), applied to the volume of exports for the relevant years, give us the overall values for the respective exports. These volumes are extrapolated to 1976. The volume of oil exports (2), from sales, is compared to the direct data for this product. For 1976, the results were as follows ($000 millions):

1. Agricultural products (unprocessed)	5.0
2. Mineral and oil products	84.2
3. Food products	1.0
4. Other light industry	0.8
5. Chemicals	5.5
6. Building Materials	0.1
7. Metal products	0.3
Total	*96.9*

Table 7
Structure of Local Final Demand (% and $000 Millions, 1976)

Sectors	(1) Value of Labour Power %	(2) Value of Labour Power $000 millions	(3) Surplus Consumption $000 millions	(4) Household Consumption %	(5) Household Consumption $000 millions	(6) Administrative Expenditure	(7) Gross Fixed Capital Formation
1. Raw Agricultural Products	26.2	6.4	4.2	20.0	10.6	—	—
2. Energy, oil, mining	2.0	0.5	1.6	4.0	2.1	1.5	—
3. Foodstuffs	41.8	10.2	8.3	34.8	18.5	1.3	—
4. Other light industry	13.9	3.4	3.5	13.1	6.9	4.5	—
5. Chemicals	5.3	1.3	1.3	4.9	2.6	—	—
6. Building Materials	—	—	—	—	—	—	—
7. Metals, engineering	3.3	0.8	1.3	4.0	2.1	1.7	17.0
8. Construction, public works	1.2	0.3	0.7	1.9	1.0	1.2	19.0
9. Transport, communications	1.2	0.3	0.8	2.1	1.1	1.3	—
10. Trade	—	—	—	—	—	—	—
11. Services	4.9	1.2	2.8	7.6	4.0	3.1	—
Public and Private	—	—	4.0	7.6	4.0	13.0	—
Total	*100.0*	*24.4*	*28.5*	*100.0*	*52.9*	*27.6*	*36.0*

Notes: Columns (4) and (5): Average per capita consumption was established at $370, and at $1,400 per economically active individual. Various studies of consumption provide the figures for distribution according to function (foodstuffs, housing, equipment, maintenance, clothing, transport, communications, leisure, education, etc.) and by sector (1 to 11 plus domestic service) around a median of $370. This came out as 68% for foodstuffs (sectors 1 to 3) 25% for sundry goods (sectors 2, 4, 5 and 7), 19% for services (sectors 8, 9 and 11).

Columns (1) and (2): The structure of distribution of income consumed was such that the poorest 50% accounted for only 23% of consumption. This consumption, $170 per capita and $645 per economically active individual, we took as representing the value involved in reproducing labour power. In the social category generated around this figure of $170 per capita, the percentages for foodstuffs, sundry goods and services came out as 68%, 25% and 7.4%, respectively.

Column 3: Surplus consumption is obtained from the difference between Columns 5 and 2.

Column 6: The distribution of administrative expenditure (salaries: 47%; goods and services: 53%) distributed proportionately within Column 6 was obtained as an average of the figures budgeted by the main Arab countries.

Column 7: The distribution of Gross Fixed Capital Formation (buildings, housing and works 53%, machinery and transport equipment — 47%) was based on the averages emerging from the national accounts of the main countries.

Figure 8
Distribution Patterns of Income Consumed

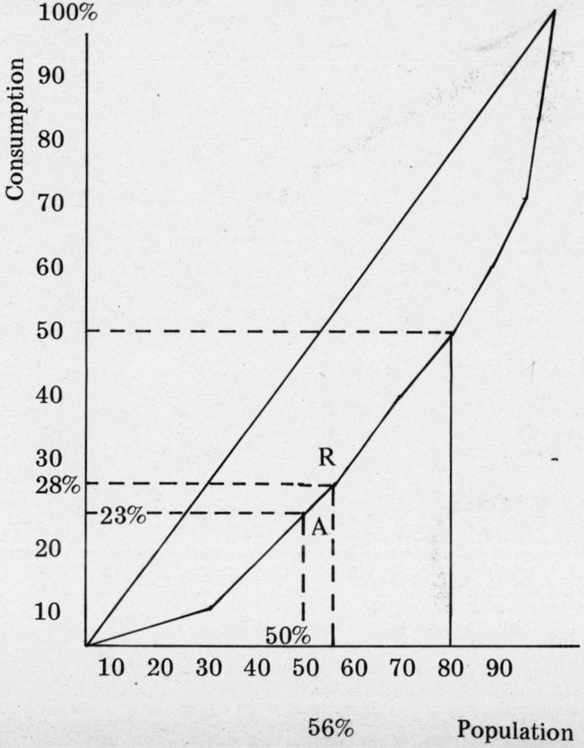

Note
The Gini curve presented here was drawn up on the basis of a 1972 Egyptian study of consumption and distribution (Source: Ghali Shoukry, Arabic edition, p.81).
The rural population accounts for 56% of the total population. If rural incomes ($14,700m) were entirely consumed, they would represent 28% of total consumption ($52,900m). Of course, inequalities exist within the rural sector itself, but the Gini curve should none the less pass close to point R. Point A, which indicates the value of labour power, is thus unlikely to be very incorrectly placed.

Table 9
Technical Coefficients

Outputs / Inputs	1	2	3	4	5	6	7	8	9	10	11
Inputs											
1. Agriculture	17	—	43	—	—	—	—	—	—	—	—
2. Energy, mining	2	10	2	2	4	9	12	4	18	—	2
3. Agro-industry	—	—	34	46	—	—	—	—	—	—	6
4. Other light industry	1	—	2	5	—	—	4	—	—	4	2
5. Chemicals	5	1	2	2	4	9	8	1	4	4	4
6. Building Materials	—	—	—	—	21	—	—	18	—	—	—
7. Metals, engineering	3	3	2	5	7	9	47	23	4	8	6
8. Construction, public works	—	—	—	—	—	—	—	—	—	4	1
Intermediate consumption	27	13	83	61	35	27	69	50	26	19	20
Value added	73	87	17	39	65	63	31	50	78	81	80
Production (total)	100	100	100	100	100	100	100	100	100	100	100

Sources and Notes:
The table was drawn up on the basis of tables for intersectorial relations for the main Arab countries.
Consumption in agriculture: (1) seed, cattlefood; (5) fertilizer.
Consumption in energy production (electricity), mining (phosphates, iron ore and other metals), water and oil extraction: mainly energy.
Consumption in agricultural and food-processing industries: (1) raw produce (grapes, wheat, vegetables and fruits, olives, cotton), animals (meat and leather); (3) carded cotton for pressing, etc.
Consumption in other light industries, mainly textiles; (3) spun thread for weaving, etc.
Consumption in chemicals industry: (6) phosphates for fertilizers.
Consumption in building materials: (2) quarry products.
Consumption in base metals (steelmaking especially) and engineering (including assembly and maintenance): (7) steel to engineering works, spare parts, etc.
Consumption in construction and public works: (6) materials (cement, etc.); (7) engineering, steel rods, etc.
Consumption in transport: (2) energy (oil).
Consumption in trade: (4) packing; (5) preservatives, plastics, (8) rents.
Consumption in services: (3) products for restaurants; (7) equipment; (8) rents.
Upkeep of buildings has been considered under Gross Fixed Capital Formation, with the exception of the rentable value of trade and services buildings.

Table 10
Margins in Trade, Transport and Services

	1	*2*	*3*	*4*	*5*	*6*	*7*
Sectors ($000 millions)							
1. Intermediate consumption[1]	5.4	12.6	17.2	5.7	1.0	0.3	3.4
2. Value added	14.7	82.1	3.6	3.6	1.9	0.8	1.7
3. Production (1 + 2)	20.1	94.7	20.8	9.3	2.9	1.1	5.1
4. Imports	4.0	6.5	4.5	3.2	6.0	2.5	24.5
5. Resources (3 + 4)	24.1	101.2	25.3	12.5	8.9	3.6	29.6
Margins							
a) %	13	3.7	20	20	20	20	20
b) $000 millions	3.1	3.7	5.1	2.5	1.8	0.7	5.9
of which: Trade	3.0	1.0	4.4	2.0	1.6	0.5	5.6
Transport[2]	0.1	2.0	0.3	0.1	0.1	0.1	0.2
Services[3]	—	0.7	0.4	0.4	0.1	0.1	0.1

Notes:

1. Intermediate consumption figures are for products 1 to 8. The 20% gross trading margins (including transport) emerge from the various intersectorial tables. The ratio is more or less the same for both local goods and imports, and from sector to sector, the only exceptions being agriculture (subsistence consumption), oil and electricity.

2. Transport: the big 'consumers' are mining products, construction works, and trade.

3. Services: mainly research and financial services, shared out between the oil industry (2), the various other industries (3 to 8), transport (9), trade (10) and services (insurance, etc.) (11).

Table 11
Inter-Sectorial Exchanges, 1976 ($000 millions)

	Intermediate Consumption								
	1	*2*	*3*	*4*	*5*	*6*	*7*	*8*	*9*
Input	*Agriculture*	*Mining, energy, oil*	*Agricultural and food-processing industry*	*Other light industry*	*Chemicals*	*Building materials*	*Metals, engineering*	*Construction, public works*	*Transport, communications*
1. Agriculture	3.4	—	8.9	—	—	—	—	—	—
2. Mining, energy, oil	0.3	9.2	0.3	0.2	0.1	0.6	0.7	1.8	—
3. Agricultural and food-processing industry	—	—	7.1	4.3	—	—	—	—	—
4. Other light industries	0.1	—	0.3	0.5	—	—	—	0.8	—
5. Chemicals	1.0	0.9	0.3	0.2	0.1	0.1	0.4	0.2	0.
6. Building materials	—	—	—	—	—	—	—	3.7	—
7. Metals, engineering	0.6	2.5	0.3	0.5	2.0	0.1	2.4	4.8	0.
8. Construction, public works	—	—	—	—	—	—	—	—	—
9. Transport, communications	0.1	2.0	0.3	0.1	0.1	0.2	1.2	—	2.
10. Trade	3.0	1.0	4.4	2.0	1.6	0.5	5.6	—	—
11. Services, public & private	—	0.7	0.4	0.4	0.1	0.1	0.1	0.4	0.
	—	—	—	—	—	—	—	—	—
A. Total Intermediary Consumption	8.5	16.3	22.3	8.2	2.8	1.0	9.3	11.8	3.
B. Value added	14.7	82.1	3.6	3.6	1.9	0.8	1.7	10.0	7.
C. Total output	23.2	98.4	25.9	11.8	4.7	1.8	11.0	21.8	10.
D. Imports	4.0	6.5	4.5	3.2	6.0	2.5	24.5	—	—
E. Total for all resources	27.2	104.9	30.4	15.0	10.7	4.3	35.5	21.8	10.

10	11	Total	*Final Demand* 1	2	3	4	5	6	7	8
Trade	*Services, public & private*	*Total Intermediate Consumption*	*Luxury Consumption*	*Necessary Consumption*	*Total Household Consumption (1 + 2)*	*Public Consumption*	*Fixed Gross Capital Formation*	*Exports*	*Total*	*Adjustment (E − 7)*
—	—	12.3	6.4	4.2	10.66	—	—	5.0	27.9	−0.7
—	0.2	13.5	0.5	1.6	2.1	1.5	—	84.2	101.3	+3.6
—	0.7	12.1	10.2	8.3	18.5	1.3	—	1.0	32.9	−2.5
0.4	0.2	2.3	3.4	3.5	6.9	4.5	—	0.8	14.5	0.5
0.5	0.4	4.5	1.3	1.3	2.6	—	—	5.5	12.6	−1.9
—	—	4.3	—	—	—	—	—	0.1	4.4	−0.1
1.1	0.6	13.5	0.8	1.3	2.1	1.7	17.0	0.3	34.6	0.9
0.6	0.1	0.7	0.3	0.7	1.0	1.2	19.0	—	21.9	−0.1
2.5	0.2	6.8	0.3	0.8	1.1	1.3	—	—	9.2	1.4
—	—	18.1	—	—	—	—	—	—	18.1	−0.9
1.2	1.1	5.3	1.2	2.8	4.0	3.1	—	—	12.4	−0.2
—	—	—	—	(4.0)	(4.0)	(13.0)	—	—	—	—
6.3	3.5	93.4	24.4	28.5	52.9	27.6	36.0	96.9	289.8	0
10.9	8.7	145.2								
7.2	12.2	238.6								
—	—	51.2								
7.2	12.2	289.8								

Table 12
Non-Agricultural Employment (000s).

	Extractive Industries, Electricity, Water	*Manufacturing Industries*	*Construction*	*Trade*	*Transport*	*Various Services*
Algeria (1966)	32	163	129	152	88	338
Morocco (1971)	99	369	11	277	15	519
Tunisia (1975)	39	241	141	120	57	379
Libya (1973)	22	22	89	37	44	189
Egypt (1975)	59	1,296	248	842	420	1974
Sudan (1971)	n.a.	370	44	155	44	866
Jordan (1961)	11	33	40	31	12	53
Syria (1976)	30	276	204	187	114	373
Lebanon (1971)	36	95	6	92	38	18
Iraq (1972)	16	160	69	155	154	603
Saudi Arabia (1966)	26	41	103	10	44	23
Kuwait (1970)	41	332	7	29	12	4
Bahrain (1971)	4	4	10	8	8	23
Arab Emirates (1968)	3	3	20	8	8	21
Oman (1972)	5	0	6	0	0	15
Yemen (1972)	0	12	n.a.	n.a.	289	225

Sources and Notes:
Labour Statistics, 1978 *(Geneva, International Labour Organization)*, *A. Brahimi*, *Dimensions et perspectives du monde arabe* (Economica, 1977), (pp. 15 and 16) and Casadio, op. cit., (p.31). Some of the statistics are manifestly wrong and we have therefore corrected them by analogy with countries with similar structures which provide more accurate statistics. We then extrapolated to 1976, to take sectorial growth into account: this gives us Table 13.

Table 13
Employment in the Arab World as a Whole (1976)

Sector	Employment (000)		Value Added ($000m)		Value Added Per Economically Active Individual ($)	
1. Agriculture	37,000		14.7		400	
2. Energy, mines	450		82.1		18,000	
3. Agro-industry	1,170		3.6		3,100	
4. Other light industry	1,170	3,500	3.6		3,100	3,300
5. Chemicals	480		1.9	11.6	4,000	
6. Building Materials	210		0.8		3,800	
7. Metals, engineering	470		1.7		3,600	
8. Construction, public works	1,700		10.0		5,900	
9. Transport	1,400		7.2		5,100	
10. Trade	2,200		10.9		5,000	
11. Services	2,100		8.7		4,100	
Administration	2,400	7,150	13.0		5,400	
Domestic	2,650		4.0		1,500	
Total	*53,400*		*162.2*		*3,000*	

Notes:
The extrapolations in Table 12 give figures for total employment in Sectors 3 to 7, and 11 to 13. The hypotheses used to establish the per capita distribution of products within manufacturing industries enable us to work out employment levels. The known figures for administration are subtracted, to give the figure for services, and a different hypothesis is used to establish the number of domestic staff. Total employment is for 1977 (Table 1), reduced by 2%.

Table 14
Number of Workers by Qualifications, Arab World as a Whole, 1976
(000 Jobs)

Sectors	*Unqualified and Lower Level Qualifications*	*Middle Level Qualifications*	*Higher Qualifications*	*Total*
1. Agriculture	37,000	—	—	37,000
2. Mines, oil	316	94	40	450
3. Agro-industry	808	259	103	1,170
4. Other light industries	808	259	103	1,170
5. Chemicals	334	103	43	480
6. Building Materials	150	43	17	210
7. Metals, engineering	324	103	43	470
8. Construction, public works	1,478	135	87	1,700
9. Transport	867	402	145	1,400
10. Trade	475	1,065	660	2,200
11. Services	570	925	610	2,100
Administration	640	1,060	700	2,400
Domestic	2,650	—	—	2,650
Total	*46,420*	*4,448*	*2,551*	*53,400*

Sources and Notes:
I.L.O. Yearbook, 1978, pp. 131ff.; Amin, *The Maghreb in the Modern World*. The percentages for lower, middle and higher level qualifications (87%, 8.3% and 4.8% respectively) correspond to educational output (illiterate or primary only, secondary or technical, tertiary). The 4.8% figure for the higher level tallies closely with the figures for Egypt and Tunisia, 1975–76 (*I.L.O. Yearbook*). Furthermore, taken together, the salaries of the low-paid and the incomes of the smaller producers represent about 50% of G.D.P.; the figure is thus compatible with the figures given for the distribution of consumption and our estimates as to the value of labour power involved. Percentages for industry, trade and services are based on the example of the Maghreb.

Table 15
Elements for Calculation of the Allocation of Labour Power

Matrix A	*1*	*2*	*3*	*4*	*5*	*6*	*7*	*8*	*9*	*10*	*11*	*Final Demand ($000 Million)* *D1*	*D2*	*D3*	*D*
1	14.7	—	33.3	—	—	—	—	—	—	—	—	6.4	4.2	1.0	11.6
2	1.3	9.4	1.1	1.7	2.2	5.5	5.5	3.2	17.0	—	1.6	0.5	1.6	79.2	81.3
3	—	—	26.5	36.3	—	—	—	—	—	—	5.7	10.2	8.3	−2.2	16.3
4	0.4	—	1.1	4.2	—	—	—	3.7	—	2.3	1.6	3.4	3.5	2.1	9.0
5	4.2	0.9	1.1	1.7	2.2	5.5	3.6	0.9	3.8	2.9	3.3	1.3	1.3	−0.5	21
6	—	—	—	—	12.8	—	—	17.0	—	—	—	—	—	−2.4	−2.4
7	2.6	2.5	1.1	4.2	4.4	5.5	21.8	22.0	3.8	6.4	4.9	0.8	1.3	4.5	6.6
8	—	—	—	—	—	—	—	—	—	3.5	0.8	0.3	0.7	20.2	21.2
9	0.4	2.0	1.1	0.9	2.2	5.5	1.8	5.6	—	14.5	1.6	0.3	0.8	1.3	2.4
10	12.8	1.0	16.5	16.8	34.0	27.8	47.3	—	—	—	—	—	—	—	—
11	—	0.7	1.5	3.4	2.2	5.5	0.9	1.8	7.5	7.0	9.0	1.2	2.8	3.1	7.1
												24.4	*24.5*	*106.3*	*155.2*
Employment per $000 million of output	1,600.0	4.55	45.0	99.0	99.6	116.4	42.4	78.2	133.7	129.0	172.3				
E1	1,600.0	3.18	31.2	68.5	69.5	83.0	29.2	68.0	82.0	27.5	46.8				
E2	0	0.96	10.0	21.8	21.2	24.0	9.3	6.2	38.0	62.0	75.5				
E3	0	0.41	3.8	8.7	8.9	9.4	3.9	4.0	13.7	39.5	50.0				

Notes:

1. Matrix A: square matrix of technical coefficients (11 sectors).
2. Final demand in $000 millions: D1 reproduction of labour power; D2 surplus consumption; D3 indirect demand (administration, gross fixed capital formation, exports less imports); D total.
3. Employment vectors: '000 jobs per $000 million production in each sector. E1 unqualified; E2 middle-level qualifications; E3 higher-level qualifications; E total.

Calculation: $/E//1 - A/^{-1} = /T/$ where T is the matrix of quantity of direct and indirect labour per $000 million of final demand.

Table 16
Intersectorial Relations, Five-Sector Aggregate

Outputs	*1*	*2*	*3*	*4*	*5*	*Total*	*Labour Power*	*Surplus Consumption*	*Admin.*	*Gross Fixed Capital Formation*	*Exports*	*Adjust-ment*	*Employ-ment*
Inputs													
1. Agriculture	3.4	—	8.9	—	—	12.3	6.4	4.2	—	—	5.0	−0.7	27.2
2. Mining, energy, oil	0.3	9.2	7.3	0.7	2.0	13.5	0.5	1.6	1.5	—	84.2	3.6	104.9
3. Industry	1.7	3.4	17.4	9.5	4.7	36.7	15.7	14.4	7.5	17.0	7.7	−3.1	95.9
4. Construction, public works	—	—	—	—	0.7	0.7	0.3	0.7	1.2	19.0	—	−0.1	21.8
5. Transport and communications	3.1	3.7	16.0	1.6	5.8	30.2	1.5	3.6	4.4	—	—	0.3	40.0
Intermediate consumption	8.5	16.3	43.6	11.8	13.2	93.4	24.4	24.5	14.6	36.0	96.9	0	289.8
Value added	14.7	82.1	11.6	10.0	26.8	145.2							
Production	23.2	98.4	55.2	21.8	40.0	238.6							
Imports	4.0	6.5	40.7	—	—	51.2							
Resources	27.2	104.9	95.9	21.8	40.0	289.8							
Employment:													
Lower-level qualifications	37,000	316	2,424	1,478	1,912	43,130							
Middle-level qualifications	—	94	767	135	2,373	3,360							
Higher-level qualifications	—	40	309	87	1,415	1,851							
Total	*37,000*	*450*	*3,500*	*1,700*	*5,700*	*48,350*							

Table 17
Allocation of Labour — Five Sectors

Matrix	*1*	*2*	*3*	*4*	*5*	*Final Demand*			
A						*D1*	*D2*	*D3*	*D*
1	14.7	—	16.2	—	—	6.4	4.2	0.3	10.9
2	1.3	9.4	2.4	3.8	5.0	0.5	1.6	82.8	84.9
3	7.3	3.4	31.5	43.5	11.7	15.7	14.4	–11.6	18.5
4	—	—	—	—	4.8	0.3	0.7	20.1	21.1
5	13.3	3.7	29.0	7.3	14.5	1.5	3.6	4.7	9.8
						24.4	24.5	96.3	145.3
Employment									
E1	1,600.0	3.18	44.0	68.0	47.8				
E2	—	0.96	13.9	6.2	59.0				
E3	—	0.41	5.6	4.0	35.2				
E	1,600.0	4.55	63.5	78.2	142.0				

Complete Bibliography of Samir Amin's Works in English and French

Introductory Notes

What follows is neither more nor less than a first attempt to construct a comprehensive bibliography of the writings of Samir Amin. Such a task seems long overdue, in view of the enormous amount that Amin has written (and continues to write). As well as providing direct references for the works cited in this book's Introduction, *The Empirical Samir Amin*, it is hoped that this will both enable and encourage readers to explore further for themselves this remarkable (and still unevenly known) body of work.

None the less, the present Bibliography can be little more than a beginning. A full, complete and accurate bibliography of Amin would surely (will, perhaps) earn somebody a Ph.D in formation science. Some of the limitations of this particular attempt are self-imposed. For one thing, it is virtually restricted to the English and French languages. It seemed unnecessary to do more than this, but impossible to do less. On the one hand, although by now Amin's work must be available in one form or another in a couple of dozen languages, these are in virtually all cases translations of French originals. (The only exceptions are one or two early works written originally in Arabic, and these have been included.)[1] The cut-off point is the end of 1980.

Conversely, the original intention of citing only such of Amin's work as was available *in English* proved unsustainable: it really is only the tip of the iceberg, and even those with no command of French ought to be given some impression of the scope and range of the *oeuvre* as a whole.

There are also constraints of a different kind. A delicate way of putting it would be to suggest that Amin has not in fact written quite so much (although nearly) as he appears to have. Perhaps inevitably, there is considerable repetition of themes. More seriously for the bibliographer, the *same* article (identically, or virtually) may turn up in different places, perhaps under slightly altered titles. It is a wearying business tracking such things down. Even the enormous benefit of having access to Amin's own compiled and oft-updated lists of his writings — without which this bibliography would scarcely have got off the ground — was considerably mitigated by the fact that even there Amin totally fails to cross-reference his own work; whether it be different languages, or different places of publishing the same article.

The bibliographer is thus inevitably cast back upon her/his own knowledge and resources. My own are very unevenly spread. It would not be too inaccurate to declare with a certain amount of confidence that most of the cross-references, doubling back, etc., have been spotted up to about 1975. But thereafter I am much less comprehensively familiar, especially with the recent French material, and I am sure that among the plethora of Amin's articles from the last few years on 'self-reliance' and kindred themes, there are bound to be duplications even among papers here listed separately.

At the risk of appearing cantankerous about this, I would like to mention one or two of the more bizarre traps that Amin has laid for the bibliographer. It may not be entirely his own fault: at all events the three publishers (two French, one English) of his two volumes of collected essays[2] have accepted standards of editing which can only be called disgraceful. In one case, no information at all is given about details of previous publications of the individual pieces; while the other makes a derisory stab at about half of them — *and* gets several wrong.

Yet no one but Amin himself, presumably, can be held responsible for what may be termed his 'autoplagiarism'. This has taken several forms. Material previously published in article form may be incorporated *verbatim* (but unacknowledged) in his books.[3] There are also two major cases of 'autoplagiarism' *between* two (or even three!) of Amin's books themselves. We have already noted in our Introduction, but it bears repeating, Brewer's comment on Amin's two best known and major theoretical works, *Accumulation on a World Scale* (AWS) and *Unequal Development* (UD): 'These two works cover virtually identical ground, and UD is perhaps better regarded as a second edition of AWS . . . Substantial passages are taken virtually unchanged from AWS and incorporated in UD.'[4] Recently (in the Introduction to his *Class and Nation*), Amin himself described UD as a 'rewrite' of AWS.[5] One wonders why he did not say this at the time (just as one wonders why AWS has footnotes and bibliography but no index, while UD has no footnotes but does have an index; and there is much more of the same kind).

The second case is still more complex and curious, involving three 'separate' works and the use of pseudonyms. Doubtless valid political reasons drove Samir Amin to use a pseudonym for his first book, *L'Egypte Nasserienne* by 'Hassan Riad':[6] a highly critical account of his own country, where he had worked for three years in government service as an economist after graduation. Similar considerations presumably prompted him to don the mantle of 'Ahmad El Kodsy' a few years later for his more general essay on 'Nationalism and Class

Struggles in the Arab World'.[7] But it does get complicated when 'El Kodsy' *quotes* from 'Riad', with approval and at length (he also cites Samir Amin).[8]

Yet this is simple compared with the denouement. Samir Amin's *The Arab Nation*, published in his own name, simply incorporates the whole of 'El Kodsy' without a word of mention or explanation (in effect *verbatim*, albeit with additions).[9] The Foreword to *The Arab Nation* admits to having 'drawn on' 'Hassan Riad', without unmasking him; as well as on two other works: Amin's own *The Maghreb in the Modern World*, and *La lutte de classes en Egypte* by Mahmoud Hussein.[10] (The latter, incidentally, is itself the pseudonym of *two* Egyptian economists, neither of whom — so far as I know! — is Samir Amin.) One wonders whether, or why, all this rigmarole was necessary. At all events, surely by now Samir Amin has attained a position wherein he no longer needs to conceal his identity or his opinions.

References

1. e.g. B.1.
2. B.14(e), B.15. (I go on about this at even greater length in my review of these volumes: Foster-Carter.)
3. See the examples cited in n.48 of the Introduction.
4. Brewer, (x.2.a.) p.233.
5. B.19e, p.vii.
6. B.3, cf. also 62 03 and 63 01.
7. 70 05.
8. e.g. 70 05e 2, p.21ff, and p. 58ff.
9. Compare 70 05e 2 p.1ff; with B.16e, p.10ff; and *passim*. (It must be said that neither of the publishers concerned was aware of this overlap.)
10. B.16e., p.9.

How to Use the Bibliography

The Bibliography is organized into four (very uneven) sections: I. *Books* by Samir Amin; II. *Articles*, etc. by Samir Amin; III. *Other* Works (theses, and unpublished writings); IV. *Debates* and critiques *of* Samir Amin (but not by him).

Every item mentioned has a letter and/or number reference, as follows:

I. *Books* by Amin are numbered B.1, B.2, etc. . . . B.20, in chronological order at *first* publication (normally in French).

If there is an English-language edition, this is given in the same number, *plus the letter 'e'*; thus, 10 10e; 12 12e; etc.

In the Notes to the Introduction, books are cited by these reference numbers, prefixed by *B*.

II. *Articles* and the like (including, for example, contributions to collective volumes) each have a reference number which incorporates: (1) a *year date* (1955 . . . . 1980); and (2) a unique number within that year (e.g., 1969 05, 1973 07). (N.B. there is no warranty, nor indeed likelihood, that *within* a given year the items are listed in precise order of publication.)

Each item has been categorized under the year of its *first* (traceable) publication; even though subsequent reproductions, translations, etc. may well be dated a year or two later than that.

As with books, the existence of an English-language version is indicated by adding an 'e' after the number. (In a few cases of articles seemingly published *first* in English and only later in French, the letter 'f' has been used for the latter.)

Where the same article has been published in more than one place, this is indicated by a *third* number. E.g. 72 01 1, 72 01 2, 72 01 3, etc. The 72 01 denotes that it is still the same paper, and the final digit merely distinguishes different sources (as often with Amin).

III. *Other Works* are cited as: T 1, T 2, T 3 (theses), U 1, U 2, . . . etc. (unpublished).

IV. *Debates*, critiques, etc. are each numbered in alphabetical order. In the Notes to the Introduction they are given the prefix 'x'; e.g. x 2, x 4, etc.

Important Note: If a reference contains (e) — i.e. 'e' in brackets — rather than just plain 'e', this means that in this specific context one can refer interchangeably to *either* English *or* French editions. Conversely, the absence of a bracket, in the Notes to the Introduction, usually means that a particular page reference in the English edition is being cited.

I Books

B: 1. *Dirasa fil tayarat al naqdia wal malia fi Micr am 1957* (Etude des flux monetaires et financiers en Egypte en 1957), Centre des Hautes Etudes arabes, Ligue arabe, Le Caire, 1959.

2. *Comptes economiques de la Republique du Mali en 1959*

Bamako and Paris, 1961; plus : *Comptes economiques 1962*, Bamako, 1962.
3. [Hassan Riad,] *L'Egypte nasserienne*, Paris, Editions de Minuit, 1964. (Also in Spanish translation).
4. *Trois experiences africaines de developpement: le Mali, la Guinee et le Ghana*, Paris, P.U.F., 1965.
5. *L'economie du Maghreb*, Paris, Ed. de Minuit, 1966; vol. I: *La colonisation et la decolonisation;* vol. II: *Les perspectives d'avenir.* (Also in Polish translation).
6. *Le developpement du capitalisme en Cote d'Ivoire*, Ed. de Minuit, 1967; 2nd edition with a Postscript, 1971.
7. *Le monde des affaires senegalais*, Paris, Ed. de Minuit, 1969, (Also in Japanese translation).
8. *Du Congo francais a l'U.D.E.A.C. —Histoire economique de l'Afrique equatoriale 1880-1968*, Paris — Dakar, Anthropos-IFAN, 1970, in collaboration with Catherine Coquery.
9. *Le Maghreb Moderne*, Paris, Ed. de Minuit, 1970.
9e. *The Maghreb in the Modern World*, Harmondsworth, Penguin, 1970.
10. *L'Afrique de l'Ouest bloquee: l'economie politique de la colonisation 1880-1970, Paris, Ed. de Minuit, 1971.*
10e. *Neocolonialism in West Africa*, Harmondsworth, Penguin, 1973.
11. *L'accumulation a l'echelle mondiale: Critique de la theorie du sous-developpement*, Dakar/Paris IFAN-Anthropos, 1970; 2nd edition with a postscript, 1971.
11e. *Accumulation on a World Scale*, (2 volumes) New York. Monthly Review Press, 1974. (Also in Spanish, Italian, Arabic, Swedish, Greek, Serbo-Croat, and Japanese translation).
12. *Le developpement inegal*, Paris, Ed. de Minuit, 1973; 2nd edition, 1974.
12e. *Unequal Development*, New York, Monthly Review Press, and Hassocks (U.K.), Harvester Press, 1976. (Also in Arabic, Spanish, German, Portuguese, Greek, and Italian translation).
13. *L'echange inegal et la loi de la valeur*, Paris/Dakar, 1963, with a contribution by J.C. Saigal, (New edition, with additions, 1981).
13e. 'The End of a Debate', Part IV in 14e (below). (Also in Italian, Spanish, and Arabic translation).
14. *L'imperialisme et le developpement inegal*, Paris, Ed. de Minuit, 1976.
14e. *Imperialism and Unequal Development* (includes 'The End of a Debate'), New York, Monthly Review Press,

and Hassocks (U.K.), Harvester Press, 1977. (Also in Portuguese and Greek translation).
15. *Imperialisme et sous-developpement en Afrique*. Paris, Anthropos, 1976.
16. *La nation arabe: nationalisme et luttes de classes.* Paris, Ed. de Minuit, 1976.
16e. *The Arab Nation*, London, Zed, 1978. (Also in Arabic translation).
17. *Eloge du socialisme*, Lithographies de Paul Rebeyrolle, Ed. Maeght, 1976.
17e. 'In Praise of Socialism', Ch. 3. in 14e (above).
18. *La loi de la valeur et le materialisme historique*, Paris Ed. de Minuit, 1977.
18e. *The Law of Value and Historical Materialism*, New York, Monthly Review Press, 1978. (Also in Portuguese and Greek translation).
19. *Classe et Nation dans l'histoire et la crise contemporaine*, Paris, Minuit, 1979.
19e. *Class and Nation, Historically and in the current crisis*, New York, Monthly Review Press, and London, Heinemann, 1980. (Also in Spanish translation).
20. *L'economie arabe contemporaine*, Paris, Minuit 1980.
20e. *The Contemporary Arab Economy*, London, Zed Press, 1982.

II: Articles, Papers, etc.

1955:

55 01 [Said El Masry] 'Ou va l'Egypte,' *Democratie Nouvelle*, 1955.

1956:

56 01 [Pierre Dupont] Problemes actuels de l'economie egyptienne, *Economie et Politique*, no. 26, 1956.

1958:

58 01 L'Economie et les Finances de la Syrie et des pays arabes, *Damas*, 1958-1960 (series of 7 articles)

a) 'Les facteurs qui conditionnent la circulation fiduciaire en Egypte' (No 20, aout 1959);
b) 'Les flux monetaires et financiers en Egypte' (No 22, octobre 1959);
c) 'Le commerce et l'exportation du coton en Egypte' (No 24, decembre 1959);
d) 'L'industrie textile en Egypte' (No 28, avril 1960);
e) 'Le programme d'industrialisation de l'Egypte' (No 29, mai 1960);

f) 'Le marche des produits pharmaceutiques' (No 31, juillet 1960);
g) 'Les industries extractives et le petrole' (No 34, octobre 1960).

58 02 Forces inflationnistes et forces deflationnistes dans l'economie egyptienne,' *Egypte contemporaine*, octobre 1958.

1959:

59 01 'Le financement des investissements dans la province egyptienne de la R.A.U.,' [*L'Egypte contemporaine*, No 297 et 299] Cairo, 1959 and 1960.

1960:

50 01 [Said el Masry] 'Le nasserisme,' *Democratie Nouvelle*, 1960.

60 02 [Yves Durelle] 'Structures et developpement de l'economie egyptienne', *Economie et Politique*, No 72, 1960.

60.03 'Pression demographique et stratification sociale dans les campagnes egyptiennes', groupe d'etudes de l'IEDES, *Tiers Monde*, No 3, 1960.

1961:

61 01 [Anon] 'L'exploitation du petrole en Egypte,' *Revue de Droit contemporain*, decembre 1961.

1962:

62.01 *Les bases d'etablissement d'une comptabilite nationale*, Centre d'Etudes de Planification socialiste, EPHE, Paris, 1962, roneote.

62 02 'Le commerce exterieur de la Republique du Mali,' *Bulletin mensuel de la E.C.E.A.O.*, juillet 1962.

62 03 [Hassan Riad] 'Les trois ages de la societe egyptienne,' *Partisans*, No. 7, 1962, No. 8, 1963.

1963:

63 01 [Hassan Riad] 'En Egypte, societe militaire et capitalisme d'Etat', *Revolution*, No. 1, 2, 1963.

63 01e 'State Capitalism in Egypt,' *Revolution*, No. 6, 1963.

63 02 [Anon] 'La lutte des classes en Afrique,' *Revolution*, No. 3, 1963.

63 02 2 Collected (Pt. III, ch. 1) in *ISDA* (B.15, above).

63 02 e1 'The Class Struggle in Africa', *Revolution*, No. 9, 1964, pp. 23-47.

63 02 e2 (Reproduced). Africa Research Group, *Reprint 2* Cambridge, Mass. 1963.

1967:

67 01 1 Le commerce interafricain,' in *Le Mois en Afrique*, No. 24, decembre 1967.

67 01 2 Collected (Pt. II, Ch. V) in *ISDA* (B.15. above).

67 01 1 'Le developpement du capitalisme en Afrique noire, in *L'Homme et la Societe*, no. 6, 1967, pp.107-119.

67 02 2 In Victor Fay ed., *En Partant du Capital.* Paris, Anthropos, 1968.
67 02 3 Collected (Pt. I, Ch. III) in *ISDA* (B.15, above).
67 02 4 Incorporated into *AAEM* (B.11, above), pp. 344-58.

1969:

69 01 1 'Pour un amenagement du systeme monetaire des pays africains de la zone franc,' *Le mois en Afrique*, No. 41, mai 1969, pp. 18-45.
69 01 2 Collected (Pt. III, Ch. VII) in *ISDA* (B.15, above).
69 02 1 'La bourgeoisie d'affaires senegalaise,' *L'Homme et la Societe*, No. 12, 2eme trimestre, 1969.
69 02 2 Collected (Pt I. Ch. IV) in *ISDA* B.15, above).
69 03 'Sous-developpement et marche international: l'experience africaine,' *Politique aujourd'hui*, Paris, aout-septembre 1969.
69 04 'Niveau des salaires, choix des techniques de production et repartition du revenu: la theorie confrontee a l'experience africaine,' in: *Les problemes des salaires dans le developpement economique*, A.D. Smith, Cahier 10, Institut International d'Etudes Sociales, Librairie Sociale et Economique, Paris, 1969.
69 04 e 'Levels of remuneration, factor proportion and income differentials, with special reference to developing countries,' in *Wage Policy Issues in Economic Development*, Ed. by Anthony D. Smith, London, Macmillan, 1969.
69 05 'L'ideologie des harmonies universelles et la theorie de l'equilibre de la balance des paiements exterieurs,' *Annales de la Faculte de Droit et des Sciences Economiques*, Dakar, 1969.
70 01 1 'Le commerce international et les flux internationaux de capitaux,' *L'Homme et la Societe*, No. 15, ler trimestre 1970.
70 01 2 Incorporated into *AAEM* (B.11, above), pp.53-65, 69-82, 104-9.
70 02 1 'Les limites de la revolution verte,' *CERES*, revue mensuelle de la F.A.O., juillet 1970 (vol. 3 No. 4).
70 02 2 Collected (Pt. II, Ch. VI) in *ISDA* (B.15, above).
70 03 [Pierre Amon] 'La revolution culturelle et le marxisme,' *Que faire*, No. 5, 1970.
70 04 'L'evolution des structures du financement du developpement economique en Egypte de 1952 a 1967,' in: *Studies in the economic history of the Middle East*, ed. by M.A. Cook, Oxford. Oxford University Press, 1970.
70 05 e1 [Ahmad El Kodsy] 'Nationalism and Class Struggles in the Arab World,' *Monthly Review*, No 3, 1970.
70 05 e2 (Collected in:) *The Arab World and Israel*, by Ahmad

El Kodsy and E. Lobel, New York. Monthly Review Press, 1970.

70 06 e 'Capitalism and Development in Ivory Coast,' in: *African Politics and Society*, ed. by Irving Leonard Markovitz, The Free Press, New York, 1970.

70 07 e1 'Development and structural change: The African experience 1950-1970,' *Journal of International Affairs*, Vol. 24, No. 2, 1970, pp. 203-225.

70 07 e2 Collected in *The widening gap, development in the 1970's*, ed. Barbara Ward, Leonore d'Anjou and J.D. Runnals, Columbia University Press, New York, 1971.

70 07 f1 'Developpement et transformations structurelles, En partant du "Rapport Pearson"', *Tiers Monde*, No. 51, 1972.

70 07 f2 In *Economie Rurale* No. 88, avril-juin 1971.

70 07 f3 Collected (Part II, Ch. I) in *ISDA* (B.15, above).

1971:

71 01 1 [Pierre Amon] 'Revolution culturelle et dialectique du centre et de la peripherie,' *L'Homme et la Societe*, No. 21, 1971.

71 01 2 Also in *Sociologie et Revolution*, coll. 10-18, 1974.

71 02 'Un bilan du developpement economique des deux dernieres decennies en Afrique,' *Le Monde Diplomatique*, decembre 1971.

71 03 'L'Afrique de l'ouest bloquee,' *Africasia*, juin-juillet 1971.

71 04 'Bilan de la premiere decennie des independances en Afrique noire, le developpement economique,' *Presence Africaine*, numero special. 'Reflexions sur la premiere decennie des independances en Afrique noire,' 3eme trimestre 1971.

71 05 'Une croissance sans developpement', *Le Monde Diplomatique*, decembre 1971.

71 06 'La politique coloniale francais a l'egard de la bourgeoisie commercante senegalaise 1820-1960,' in: *The development of indigenous trade and markets in West Africa*, (ed.) Claude Meillassoux and Daryll Forde, Oxford. Oxford University Press, 1971.

71 07 1 Critique de livre; Serge Thion, *Le Pouvoir Pale*, in *Tiers Monde*, No. 48, octobre-decembre 1971.

71 07 2 Collected (Pt. III, Ch. III) in *ISDA* (B.15, above).

71 08 1 Critique de livre; Mario de Andrade et Marc Olivier, *La Guerre en Angola*, in *L'Homme et la Societe*, No. 22, 1971.

71 08 2 Collected (Pt. II, Ch. IV) in *ISDA* (B.15, above).

71 09 1 'L'Afrique sous-peuplee, in *Population, Education, Developpement en Afrique au Sud du Sahara*, Bureau

Regional pour l'Education en Afrique, BREDA, Dakar, dec. 1971.
71 09 2 Also in:, *Developpement et Civilisations*, No 47-48, mars-juin 1972.
71 09 3 Collected (Pt. III, Ch. V) in *ISDA* (B.15, above).
71 09 e1 'Underpopulated Africa,' *African Newsletter*, McGill University, Montreal, No. 2, 1972.
71 09 e2 Also in: *Sociology in Africa, a Book of Readings*, (ed.) P.F. Wilmot, Ahmadu Bello University, Zaria, Nigeria 2 vols., 1973.
71 09 e3 Also published by: ENI, Addis Ababa, 1973.
71 09 e4 Also in *Maji Maji*, Dar es Salaam, 1972.
71 10 *Encyclopaedia Universalis*, Paris, 1971, articles: Cote d'Ivoire,' 'Economie du Developpement,' 'Ghana', 'Guinee', 'Industrialisation,' 'Mali', 'Maroc.'
71 11 e *African Survey and Directory*, Europa Publications, London 1971, articles: Dahomey, Guinea, Ivory Coast, Mali, Mauritania, Niger, Senegal, Togo, Upper Volta.

1972:
72 01 1 'Sous-developpement et dependance en Afrique noire, les origines historiques et les formes contemporaines, preface a Boubacar Barry, *Le royaume du Walo: le Senegal avant la conquete*, Paris, Maspero, 1972.
72 01 2 Also in *Partisans*, 64, 1972.
72 01 3 Also in *Tiers Monde*, No. 52, Oct-Dec. 1972, pp. 753-78.
72 01 4 Collected (Pt. I, Ch. I) in *ISDA* (B.15, above).
72 01 e1 'Underdevelopment and dependence in Black Africa', *The Journal of Modern African Studies*, Vol. 10 No. 4, 1972, pp. 503-24.
72 01 e2 Also in: *Journal of Peace Research*, No. 2, 1972.
72 01 e3 Also in: *Social and Economic Studies*, vol. 22, 1973, University of the West Indies, Jamaica.
72 02 1 'Le modele theorique d'accumulation et de developpement dans le monde contemporain,' *Tiers Monde*, No 52, octobre-decembre 1972.
72 02 2 Also in: *Collection d'Etudes sur le developpement economique et social*, No. 1, NEA, Dakar, 1973.
72 02 3 Collected as 'Introduction' in *ISDA* (B.15, above).
72 02 e1 'Accumulation and Development, a theoretical model', *Review of African Political Economy*, No. 1, 1972.
72 02 e2 Also in: *Series in Economic and Social Development*, No. 1, NEA, Dakar, 1973.
72 02 e3 Also in Stephen S. Holphe (ed.) *Essays on the Development of Underdevelopment in Africa*, Simon and Schuster Inc., New York, 1975.
72 02 e4 Also in: *Dependency and Underdevelopment in Latin*

America and the Caribbean, University of Toronto, 1975.
72 03 1 'CNUCED III, Un bilan,' *Bulletin of Peace Proposals*, No. 3, 1972, Oslo.
72 03 2 Collected (Pt. II, Ch. 2) in *ISDA* (B.15, above).
72 03 e 'UNCTAD III, a critical appraisal,' *New Statements*, Quebec, No. 1, 1973.
72 04 1 'Zone franc et developpement', in: *Afrique et integration monetaire*, (ed.) Rodrigue Tremblay, Universite de Montreal, 1972.
72 04 2 Collected (Pt. III, Ch. VIII) in *ISDA* (B.15, above).
72 05 1 'Le developpement du bassin du fleuve Senegal' Preface a Ahmed Ould Daddah, *Contribution a l'etude du developpement des transports sur le Fleuve Senegal*, Universite de Dakar, 1972.
72 05 2 Collected (Pt. II, Ch. 9) in *ISDA* (B.15, above).
72 06 1 'Problemes actuels de l'Unite africaine', expose introductif, in: *Problemes actuels de l'unite africaine, SNED*, Alger, 1972.
72 06 2 Collected (Pt. III, Ch. VI) in *ISDA* (B.15, above).
72 07 'Quel Developpement', I.P.D., Douala, 1972.

1973:

73 01 1 'Le paradoxe africain le deficit alimentaire de l'Afrique: *CERES*, No 25, 1973.
73 01 2 Collected (Pt. II, Ch. 7) in *ISDA* (B.15, above).
73 02 'Groissance n'est pas developpement', *Forum du Developpement*, No. 3, 1973.
73 02 e 'Growth is not Development,' *Developement Forum*, No. 3, 1973.
73 03 'La dimension mondiale de la lutte des classes,' *Minuit* 3, 1973.
73 04 'L'homme et sa production,' in *Guides de Recherches, l'Afrique noire*, edite par D. Martin et T. Yannopoulo, Fondation Nationale des Sciences Politiques, Armand Colin, 1973.
73 05 e 'The place of economic history in the teaching of economics in Africa', in *The Teaching of Economics in Africa*, (ed.) Livingstone, Routh, Rweyemamu and Svendsen, Sussex University Press, 1973.
73 06 e 'Transitional Phases in Sub-Saharan Africa', *Monthly Review*, October 1973.
73 06 f Collected (Pt. II, Ch. 3) in *ISDA* (B.15, above).
73 07 'A propos de "7 theses erronees sur l'Amerique latine"', *L'Homme et la Societe*, No. 27, 1973.
73 08 'Proces intente par le Tiers Monde a l'Europe,' Institut d'Etudes Politiques, Paris.
74 01 1 'Le capitalisme et la rente fonciere,' in: S. Amin et K.

Vergopoulos, *La question paysanne et le capitalisme*, Paris/Dakar, Anthropos-IDEP, 1974.
74 01 2(e) Collected as Ch. 2, 'Capitalism and Ground Rent', in *I&UD* (B.13(e), above).
74 02 1(e) 'The migratory phenomenon in contemporary West Africa', *Modern Migrations in Western Africa*, (ed.) S. Amin, Oxford University Press, 1974. (In English *and* French).
74 02 2 Collected (Pt. II, Ch. IV) in *ISDA* (B.14, above).
74 03 1 Presentation, G.K. Amoa et O. Braun, *Echanges Internationaux et sous-developpement*, Paris/Dakar, Anthropos-IDEP, 1974.
74 03 2(e) Collected as Ch. 6, 'International Trade and Imperialism', in *I&UD* (B.13(e), above).
74 04 1 'Les problemes de l'environnement en Afrique', *Espaces et Societes*, No. 10-11, octobre 1973-fevrier 1974.
74 04 2(e) ? collected as Ch. 7, 'The Problems of the "Environment"', in *I&UD* (B.13(e), above).
74 05 'Les etapes d'evolution du capitalisme peripherique', *Economic et humanisme*, No 216, mars-avril 1974.
74 05 'La crise', *Le Monde Diplomatique*, novembre 1974.
74 07 'Europeens, soyez tiers-mondistes,' *Le Sauvage*, octobre 1974.
74 08 'Le monde peripherique', *L'economiste du Tiers Monde*, janvier 1974.
74 09 1 'Une crise structurelle', *Minuit* 9, 1974.
74 09 2 Also in Amin, Faire, Hussein et Massiah, *La crise de l'imperialisme*, Paris, Minuit, 1975.
74 09 3 Also in: *Jeune Afrique*, fevrier, 1975.
74 10 Amin, Eynard et Stuckey, 'Feminisme et lutte des classes,' *Minuit* 7, 1974.
74 11 S. Amin et I. Eynard, 'Los Angeles, U.S. of Plastika,' *L'Homme et la Societe*, No. 33-34, 1974.
74 12 'Vers une nouvelle crise structurelle du capitalisme,' *Sociologie et Societes*, No. 2, novembre 1974, Montreal.
74 12 e1 'Towards a new structural crisis of the capitalist system', in Amin and Widstrand, (ed.) *Multinational firms in Africa*, IDEP-Scandinavian Institute of African Studies, Uppsala, 1975.
74 12 e2 Also in: *Socialist Revolution*, No. 1, 1975, San Francisco.
74 13 'Eloge du Socialisme', *L'Homme et la Societe*, No. 31-32, 1974. (See B.16, above).
74 13 e 'In Praise of Socialism', *Monthly Review*, September 1974. (See B.16(e), above).
74 14 e1 'Marxism: looking backward and forward', *Monthly Review*, vol. 26 No. 2 june 1974.

74 14 (e)2 Collected as part of introduction to *I&UD* (B.13(e), above).

74 15 e1 'Modes of production and social formations', *Ufahamu*, Vol 4, No. 3, 1974.

74 15 (e)2 Incorporated in *UD* (B.12(e), above), ch. 1.

74 16 e 'Land Use, agriculture and food supply,' Introduction, in *Population in African Development*, (ed.) P. Cantrelle and others, Ordina Ed., Dolhain, Belgium 1974.

1975:

75 01 'C'est une crise d l'imperialisme,' *Minuit* 14, mai 1975.

75 02 'Autogestion yougoslave et developpement african', *Ethiopiques*, Dakar, no. 1, 1975.

75 03 'Preface a Samuel Nana Sinkam', *Pays candidats au processus de developpement*, Mouton, 1975.

75 04 1 'Le statut de la rationalite economique; la critique de la micro-economie,' in Amin, Franco et Sow, *La planification du sous-developpement*, Paris/Dakar, Anthropos/IDEP, 1975.

75 04 2(e) Collected as Ch. 1, 'Criticism of Micro-economics,' in *I&UD* (B.14(e), above).

75 05 1 'L'esclavage en Afrique'. Presentation, in Babacar Sine, *Imperialisme et theories sociologiques du developpement*, Paris/Dakar, IDEP-Anthropos, 1975.

75 05 2 Collected (Pt. III, Ch. 2) in *ISDA* (B.15, above).

75 06 'Abandonner le modele occidental de consommation,' *Le Monde*, 11 mars 1975.

75 07 'Le Tiers Monde peut-il faire front,' *Le Nouvel Observateur*, 17 fevrier 1975.

75 08 'Quelle education pour quel developpement?' *Perspectives*, No. 1, 1975, UNESCO.

75 08 e 'What education, for what development?' *Prospects*, No. 1, 1975, UNESCO.

75 09 1 'L'Association eurafricaine, quelques aspects du probleme', *Eurafrica*, avril-mai 1975.

75 09 2 ? Collected (Pt. III, Ch. IX) in *ISDA* (B.15, above).

75 10 'Une remise en cause de l'ordre international,' *Le Monde Diplomatique*, juin 1975.

75 11 'Mise au point,' *Temps Modernes*, aout-septembre 1975.

75 12 1 'Vocations universelles et aires structurelles,' *Minuit* 15, septembre 1975.

75 12 e 'Universality and Cultural Spheres', *Monthly Review*, February 1977.

75 12 2(e) Collected as Ch. 4. of *I&UD* (B.14(e), above).

75 13 e 'Response to Jonah Raskin', *Monthly Review*, No. 6, nov. 1975.

75 14 e 'The Early Roots of Unequal Exchange, *The Modern*

World System by I. Wallerstein,' *Monthly Review*, No. 7, dec. 1975.

75 14 f Collected (Pt. I, Ch. II) in *ISDA* (B.15, above).

1976:

76 01 Presentation, in Beaud, Bellon, Francois, *Lire le Capitalisme*, Anthropos, 1976.

76 01 e 'Capitalism, State Collectivism and Socialism', *Monthly Review*, June 1977, No. 2, Vol. 29.

76 02 1 'Perspectives de la localisation internationale des activites industrielles' — *Etudes de politique industrielle*, G.R.E.S.I., Ministere de l'Industrie et de la Recherche, Paris.

76 02 2 'Les perspectives internationales de la localisation industrielle, un point de vue arabo-african', *Options Mediterraneennes*, No. 36.

76 02 3 Also in: *Cahiers de la Toison d'Or*, juin 1977, Bruxelles.

76 03 1 'Le Tiers Monde et le nouvel ordre economique international,' in *Cultures*, vol. III No. 4, Les presses de l'UNESCO et la Baconniere.

76 03 2 Also in: Mamadou Dia, *Emancipation des economies captives*, Paris, Anthropos, 1976.

76 03 e 'The Third World and the New Economic Order', *Cultures*, vol. III No. 4, UNESCO.

76 04 'Reponse a un questionnaire', in A. Birou et P.M. Henry, *Pour un autre developpement*, Paris P.U.F.

76 04 e In A. Birou, P.M. Henry, & J.P. Schlegel (eds.) *Towards a Re-Definition of Development*, Oxford, Pergamon, 1977.

76 05 'A mi-chemin du dialogue Nord-Sud, Pour une strategie de rupture', *Economia*, juillet-aout 1976.

76 06 'Presentation', in Pascal Lissouba, *Conscience du developpement et democratie*, N.E.A.

76 07 'Le transfert de technologie', *Encyclopedia Universalis*, supplement Universalia.

76 07 (e) Collected as Ch. 10 of *I&UD* (B.14(e), above).

76 08 'Sept propositions pour le Tiers Monde', *Jeune Afrique*, No. 801, 14 mai 1976.

76 09 'L'art: integration ou revolte', *Minuit* 20.

76 10 'A propos de la critique', *L'homme et la Societe*, No. 39-40.

76 11 'L'alphabetisation et l'education de masse pour le developpement,' in *Confrontation pluridisciplinaire sur l'alphabetisation*, Colloque de Persepolis, ed. Leon Bataille, UNESCO.

76 11 e 'Literacy training and mass education for development', in *A Turning Point for Literacy*, (ed.) Leon Bataille,

International Coordination Secretariat for Literacy, Paris, Pergamon.
76 12 'La cooperation intellectuelle pour un nouvel ordre economique, independance ou autorcie?' *Informations UNESCO*, No. 707-708; Le Courrier de l'UNESCO.
76 12 e 'The search for a new world economic order', *UNESCO*, Courrier, oct. 1976.
76 13 'Pour un ordre economique multipolaire et democratique' *L'Ouest africain*, nov.-dec. 1976.
76 14 e 'Population and Development', *Socialist Revolution*, No. 27, January-March 1976.
76 15 e 'UNCTAD IV and the New International Economic Order,' in *Africa Development*, CODESRIA, Dakar, No. 1, 1976.
76 16 e1 'After Nairobi, Preparing the non-aligned summit in Colombo, An appraisal of UNCTAD IV in Non-alignment and Third World Solidarity,' *Marga Quarterly Journal*, vol. 3, 1976, Colombo, Sri Lanka.
76 16 e2 Also in: *Africa Development*, vol. 1 No. 2, 1976.
76 16 e3 Also in: *Journal of Contemporary Asia*, No. 3, 1976.
76 17 e1 'Social characteristics of Peripheral Formations, an Outline for a Historical Sociology,' *Berkeley Journal of Sociology*, vol. 21, 1976.
76 17 (e)2 Absorbed into *UD* (B.12(e), above), Ch. 5.
1977:
77 01 'La strategie de la revolution socialiste dans le Tiers Monde,' in *Connaissance du Tiers Monde*, Cahiers Jussieu No. 4, Universite de Paris 7, 10-18, 1977.
77 02 'Le Tiers Monde et la division internationale du travail, Autarcie ou ordre multipolaire democratique', *Le Monde Diplomatique*, fevrier 1977.
77 03 'Presentation', in Kostas Vergopoulos, *Le capitalisme difforme et la nouvelle question agraire, l'exemple de la Grece moderne*, Maspero 1977.
77 04 'Le Marxisme apres 1945', *Encyclopedie Larousse*, 1977.
77 05 'Cultures et structures precapitalistes', Interview, Pepe-huit, Paris, Universite de Vincennes, mars 1977.
77 06 e 'The future of Southern Africa', *Journal of Southern African Affairs*, Vol. II, No. 3, 1977, University of Maryland, U.S.A.
77 06 f 'Les perspectives de l'Afrique Australe,' *Tiers Monde*, Janvier-Mars 1979.
77 07 e 'A Comment on "Theories of the World" Economy and Imperialism' by Ira Gerstein, in *Insurgent Sociologist*, University of Oregon, Vol. VII No. 2, Spring 1977.
77 08 e 'Some thoughts on Self-Reliant Development, Collective Self-Reliance and the New International Economic

Order', *Journal de l'A.E.T.M.*, Alger, No. 1, 1977.
77 09 e1 'Self-Reliance and the New International Economic Order', *Monthly Review*, July-August 1977.
77 09 e2 Also in: *The Non-Aligned Movement in World Politics*, (ed.) by A.W. Singham, New York, Lawrence Hill & Co, 1978.
77 09 f1 'Developpement autocentre, autonomie collective et P.E.I.N.', *Africa Development* No. 1, 1978.
77 09 f2 Also in: *L'Occident en desarroi*, Dunod, 1978.

1978:

78 01 'Societes precapitalistes et capitalisme,' in Frank & Amin, *L'accumulation dependante*, Paris, Anthropos, 1978.
78 02 'N'attendons pas 1984;' in A.G. Frank, *Reflexions sur sur la nouvelle crise economique mondale*, Maspero 1978.
78 02 e In A.G. Frank, *Reflections on the World Economic Crisis*, New York, Monthly Review Press, London, Hutchinson, 1981.
78 03 'Developpement et Environnement,' *Tiers Monde*, janvier-mars 1978.
78 04 (e) 'L'auto-dependance collective et le nouvel ordre economique international,' *Developpement et progres socio-economique*, revue organisation de la solidarite des peuples afro-asiatiques, No. 12, 1978, Cairo. (Also English edition).
78 05 'A propos du N.O.E.I. et de l'avenir des relations economiques internationales', *Africa Development*, No. 4, 1978.
78 06 e 'Development Theory and the crisis in development'; in *Emerging Trends in Development Theory*, S.A.R.E.C. Report, Stockholm 1978.
78 07 e 'The New World Economic Order, Reaction of the Developed World and Strategy of Use of the Financial Surpluses of Certain Developing Countries in International Financing of Economic Development', Dubrovnik 1977, published Belgrade, 1978.
78 08 e1 Lessons of Kampuchea, in Ikwezi, No. 10, dec. 1978.
78 08 (e)2 Collected as Ch. 8 of *I&UD* (B.14(e), above).

1979:

79 01 'La France et le Tiers Monde', in *Vincennes ou le desir d'apprendre*, Ed. A. Moreau et U. de Paris VIII, Vincennes 1979.
79 02 'La faillite de la science bourgeoise et l'eloge du Socialisme', in *Rebeyrolle, Peintures 1968-78*, Paris 1979.
79 03 'L'avenir des relations economiques internationales,'

in *Le Dialogue Inegal*, Amin, Nyerere, Perren, CETIM, Geneve, 1979.

79 04 Postface, 'L'economie politique de l'Afrique dans la crise contemporaine', in Herve Bourges et Claude Wauthler, *Les 50 Afriques*, Tome 2, Paris, Seuil 1979.

79 05 1 'Reflexions sur la theorie de l'Imperialisme', in *Le Tiers Monde de la gauche*, Paris, Seuil 1979.

79 05 2 Also in *La France et le Tiers Monde*, PUG, 1979.

79 06 e 'Towards an alternative strategy of autocentered development', in *Transnational Corporations and World Order*, Ed. by G. Modelski, Freeman U.S.A. 1979.

79 07 'Le N.O.E.I. et l'education,' *Ethiopiques*, Dakar, Janvier 1979.

79 08 'Vers une nouvelle vague de luttes populaires,' *Le Monde Diplomatique*, Mai 1979.

79 09 'Le N.O.E.I.', *Developpement et Progres socio-economique*, Cairo, No. 1, 1979.

79 10 'La structure de classe du systeme imperialiste contemporain,' *Socialism in the World*, Belgrade, No. 12, 1979.

79 11 'Le developpement inegal et la question nationale,' *L'Homme et la Societe*, No. 51-54, Janvier-Decembre 1979.

79 12 e 'N.I.E.O.: How to put Third World Surpluses to Effective Use,' *Third World Quarterly*, Vol. 1, No. 1, Jan. 1979, London.

79 13 e 'The Third World today and the International Division of Labour', AMPO, vol. II No. 1, 1979, Tokyo. (In English).

79 14 e 'N.I.E.O. and the Strategy for the use of financial surplus of developing countries,' *Alternatives*, vol. IV No 4, March 1979.

79 15 e 'Reply to Weeks and Dore', in Views on Dependency, *Latin American Perspectives* vol. VI No 2, Spring 1979, Riverside, California.

79 16 e 'S. Amin attacks Lester Brown's Malthusianism,' *Populi*, Vol. 6, No. 4, 1979.

79 17 e 'No substitute for self centered development', *The Middle East*, July 1979.

1980:

80 01 *Three essays on world capitalism*, Nalanda House Publication Madras, 1980.

80 02 e 'Sous developpement et histoire, le cas de l'Afrique,' in *History and Underdevelopment*, Ed. by L. Blusse et Var, Leiden Centre for the history of European Expansion, Leiden 1980.

80 03 'Le contenu technologique de la self-reliance', in *Technologie et industrialisation en Afrique*, (Ed.) F. Yachir,

CODESRIA book series, Dakar 1980.
80 04 'Developpement autocentre, autonomie collective et NOEI,' in Amin, Faire, Malkin, *L'Avenir Industriel de l'Afrique*, Harmattan 1980.
80 05 e 'Collective self-reliance or National liberation', in *Dialogue for a new order*, (Ed.) K. Hag, Pergamon 1980.'
80 06 e 'Some thoughts on Methods of analysing the Modern world,' in *Social Science, For What*, (Ed.) H.H. Holm and E. Rudeng, Universitetsforlaget, Oslo 1980.
80 07 'Le NOEI — Quel avenir?' *Tiers Monde*, No. 81, Janv-Mars 80.
80 08 'Vers un nouvel ordre economique mondial,' *Alternatives non violentes*, No. 37, 1980.
80 09 'Du Rapport Pearson (1970) au Rapport Brandt (1980), ou la Crise de l'ideologie du developpement', *Africa Development* Vol. V, No 3, 1980, Dakar.
80 10 'Revolution ou decadence? La crise du systeme Imperialiste contemporain et celle de l'Empire romain.' *Review* IV, 1, Summer 1980.
80 11 'La question nationale', *L'Homme et la Societe*, No. 55-58 Janv-Dec 1980.
80 12 e 'The class structure of the imperialist system', *Monthly Review*, Janv. 1980.
80 13 e 'Concerning Eurocommunism', *Contemporary Marxism*, No. 2, 1980 (San Francisco).

III. Other Works

(a) Theses

T 01 *Les revenus susceptibles d'epargne et leur utilisation en Egypte 1938-1952.* These de Statistiques, ISUP, Paris, 1956.
02 *Les effets structurels de l'integration internationale des economies precapitalistes: une etude theorique du mecanisme qui a engendre les economies dites sous-developpees.* Doctorat d'Etat es Sciences Economiques, Paris 1957. (Prix de la Faculte de Droit et des Sciences Economiques.)
03 *Le developpement economique de la Cote d'Ivoire, 1950-65: Evaluation de la croissance et de la distribution sociale du revenu.* These complementaire pour l'agregation, Paris, 1966.

(b) Unpublished Reports, etc.

U 01 Rapports d'ensemble sur la structure de l'economie egyptienne en 1959: les banques, les institutions financieres, l'industrie textile, les autres industries, les services et les transports, les flux monetaires et financiers (In Arabic, Cairo, Al Muassassa al

Iqtisadia, 1959).
02 *Un modele financier a prix variables pour l'economie francaise*, SEEF, Ministere des Finances, Paris 1960.
03 *Le developpement des affaires privees africaines au Congo Kinshasa depuis 1958*, IDEP, 1966.
04 *Autofinancement, politique des prix et acceleration de la croissance, les lecons de la decennie 60*, Institut de Vienne pour le Developpement et la Cooperation, 1968, document roneote.
05 *Rapport sur le Congo Brazzaville* (mission d'evaluation du P.N.U.D.), Brazzaville, Ministere du Plan, 1968, document roneote. Documents annexes: *L'A.E.F., 1920-1960*, et *l'evolution des pays de l'U.D.E.A.C., 1960-1968.*
06 *Critique du projet Education et desarmement*, Centre Europeen de Coordination, de Recherche et de Documentation en Sciences Sociales, Vienne, 1968, document roneote.

IV. Debates, Critiques &c of Amin

X 1 H. Bernstein, 'Sociology of Underdevelopment vs. Sociology of Development?' In D. Lehmann (ed.) *Development Theory: Four Critical Essays* London: Frank Cass, 1978.
2(a) A.A. Brewer, 'Amin', Ch. 10 of *Marxist Theories of Imperialism* (RKP, 1980).
(b) *Idem.*, 'On Amin's Model of Autocentric Accumulation', *Capital and Class* 10, Spring 1980, pp. 114-25 (Including reply by Samir Amin. See also *corrections* in Capital and Class No. 11, Summer 1980, pp. 154-5).
3 M. Bronfenbrenner, 'Review article: a world class economist from underdeveloped Africa', *Ec. Devt. & Cult. Change* 27:1 Oct. 1978, pp. 195-201.
4 Cheng Ngai-Lung, *Underdevelopment and the World Capitalist System — an evaluation of some recent studies.* University of Salford, Dept. of Sociological and Political Studies, M.Sc. thesis, 1976; ch. 3, pp. 57-97 (pp. 84-97 compares Wallerstein and Samir Amin).
5(a) Irs Gerstein, 'Theories of the World Economy and Imperialism', *The Insurgent Sociologist*, 7:2, Spring 1977 (Special issue: *Imperialism and the State*) pp. 9-22.
(b) S. Amin, 'Comment on Gerstein', *ibid.*, pp. 99-103.
(c) N. Disney, 'Accumulation on a World scale', *ibid.*, pp. 124-8. (See also *Review*, 3.)
6 John F. Henry, 'Debate', *Rev. Afr. Pol. Ec.*, No. 4 (Nov. 1975). pp. 105-6.
6 Mohammad Ja'far, 'National Formation in the Arab Region: a critique of Samir Amin', *Khamsin* 6, 1978, pp.60-86.

8 Richard Leaver, 'Samir Amin on Underdevelopment', *J. Contemp. Asia* 9:3, 1979, pp.325-36.

9(a) Jean-Pierre Olivier, 'Afrique: qui exploite qui? (A propos de Samir Amin et des bourgeoises d'Etat africaines)'. *Les Temps Modernes*, No. 346 (May 1975) pp. 1506-51; and No. 347 (June 1975) pp. 1744-75.

(b) S. Amin, 'Mise au point', *ibid.*, No. 349-50, Aug-Sept. 1975, pp. 367-9.

(c) J. P. Olivier, 'Reponse a une mise au point', *ibid.*, No. 353, Dec. 1975, pp. 935-6.

10 Anne Phillips, 'The Concept of Development', *Rev. Af. Pol. Ec.* No. 8 (Jan-Apr. 1977), pp. 7-20 (esp. pp. 13-15).

11 Jonah Raskin/S. Amin 'In Praise of Socialism: An Exchange', *Monthly Review* 27:6, Nov. 1975, 52-9.

12 G. Rubinstein, G. Smirnov, V. Solodnikov, 'On Some Statements by Samir Amin', *Rev. Afr. Pol. Ec.* No. 5 (Jan-Apr. 1976) pp. 103-9.

13 Jonathan Schiffer, 'The Changing Post-War Pattern of Development: the accumulated wisdom of Samir Amin', *World Development* p:6 June 1981 pp. 515-37.

14(a) Sheila Smith, 'The Ideas of Samir Amin: theory or tautology?' *Jnl. Devt. Studies.* 17:1 Oct. 1980, pp. 5-21.

(b) *Idem.*, 'Chopped Logistics' [review of *Class and Nation*]. *South*, 2 Nov. 1980.

15 Aidan Foster-Carter, review of Amin [B 14, B 15] *Sociology*, vol. 13, no. 2, May 1979.